The Board
of Adjustment

The Board of Adjustment

THE CITIZENS PLANNING SERIES

V. Gail Easley, FAICP
and
David A. Theriaque

PLANNERS PRESS
AMERICAN PLANNING ASSOCIATION
Chicago, Illinois
Washington, D.C.

ISBN (paperback edition): 1-932364-02-1
ISBN (hardbound edition): 1-932364-03-X
Library of Congress Control Number: 2004116014

Printed in the United States of America

Editing and interior composition by Joanne Shwed, Backspace Ink
Index by Lowanda Tucker
Cover design by Susan Deegan

Contents

Acknowledgements

My first introduction to the discipline of planning was as a citizen planner. When the Community Development Block Grant program was created, I was appointed to the first Citizens' Advisory Committee. Later that same year, I was appointed to a regional goal-setting committee for North Central Florida. When I attended graduate school at the University of Tennessee, Jim Spencer, FAICP, impressed upon me the importance of "participating the public." It is fitting that I contribute to the ability of the citizen planner to make great communities happen.

Wayne Bennett, AICP, opened the door to expanded training for citizen planners including an idea for a program for board of adjustment members in Kentucky. From that experience, the idea for this book was born. Mike Harper, FAICP, encouraged the book and provided stories about his own experiences, one of which is described in this book.

Carol Barrett, FAICP, wrote the chapter on ethics for citizen planners (Chapter 7) while driving cross-country to a new job. Her work is a "must read" for all citizen planners.

Marion Cook and John Weil provided valuable research support. Cassie Langdon provided much of the necessary drudgery to copy, compile, and crosscheck the information.

Sylvia Lewis, Director of Publications for the American Planning Association, encouraged our efforts and exhibited great patience during the process of creating and delivering a manuscript.

This book could not have been possible without David Theriaque. He co-authored this book with painstaking attention to detail and good humor. He led the way on legal matters and provided thought-provoking critiques of my work to strengthen the final product.

Thanks to all who supported our efforts and believed in the value of the work.

V. Gail Easley, FAICP
September 2004

Foreword

Citizens are at the heart of every successful planning program. Planners are charged to serve the public interest, which is made up of the values and visions of these local citizens. Citizens are elected to lead government and plan their communities, and are appointed to commissions and boards to provide advice and make decisions in order to implement these plans. Whether they are new to the job or are seasoned veterans, these citizen planners need information and training to carry out their responsibilities.

The Kentucky Legislature had adopted a requirement that every planner—citizen and professional alike—receive training. The Professional Development Officer for the Kentucky Chapter of the American Planning Association, Wayne Bennett, wanted to put together a training program for boards of adjustment. Bennett, along with Easley and Theriaque, set out to prepare a training manual. We soon discovered that, while much had been written to provide training to planning commissioners, there was very little available to guide board of adjustment members in carrying out their responsibilities. To fill this void, Bennett, Easley, and Theriaque wrote a training manual. That experience sparked interest in writing a book that would be useful to board members everywhere.

There are 38,967 units of local government in the United States,[1] which includes 3,034 counties and 35,933 cities, towns, and townships. In some states, small cities and towns are not authorized to adopt zoning ordinances; however, the majority of local governments are engaged in land use and comprehensive planning as well as the regulation of land use and development. These local governments have planning commissions, boards of adjustment, code enforcement boards, and many other types of boards and commissions. There are hundreds of thousands of these citizens who are working together to plan and regulate the use of land in their communities.

---

1. U.S. Department of Commerce. *2002 Census of Governments, Volume 1, Number 1*, Government Organization. Washington, DC: U.S. Census Bureau, 2002.

List of Tables

List of Figures

Introducing the
Board of Adjustment

CHAPTER

1

In the Beginning

Among material resources, the greatest, unquestionably,
is the land. Study how a society uses its land, and you can come
to pretty reliable conclusions as to what its future will be.

E.F. SCHUMACHER

Land is a finite resource. As a society, we deliberate on the ways that we can and should use our land, resulting in plans for the way our cities, towns, and countryside will be used. Contemporary plan making may create plans identified with many names including "comprehensive plans," "general plans," "master plans," "land use plans," and "smart growth plans." The essential feature of most plans is direction on how land should be developed and used. Once the plan is in place, the key to its success is the implementation.

A plan is important, in part, because of the process of preparing the plan. The plan should belong to the whole community, and the people who live and work in the community should be part of the process that creates the plan. Even more important than the plan itself is whether the plan actually results in a good quality of life for its residents.

Most communities divide the various planning responsibilities among elected officials, local government staff, and citizen boards and commissions. The elected body has ultimate responsibility; however, this body delegates certain matters to staff and citizens. Typically, there is a "planning commission" (also called a "planning board" and a "planning and zoning board") with responsibilities for plan making and, depending on the locale, responsibilities for many aspects of implementation, such as zoning and site plan review. In regulations are the zoning ordinance and subdivision regulations. While subdivision regulations are primarily concerned with dividing vacant land into separate lots in order to sell the individual lots and allow development on each lot, zoning is often concerned with redevelopment matters.

The concept of zoning is relatively simple: Land in a jurisdiction is divided into districts or zones in order to regulate what kinds of uses may be located within the zone. Each zone has a specific set of permissible uses and a set of design standards. These standards regulate the location of buildings by requiring a predetermined distance from the lot line to the building edge, which is called a "setback" because the building must be set back from the lot lines on the front, sides, and rear of the lot. Typical standards set maximum limits for building height and amount of lot coverage, and minimum requirements for the amount of landscaping or parking. What happens when a lot is unusual and cannot be developed while meeting all of the standards? Zoning ordinances typically include a means of varying from the required standards, which is called a "variance" or a "waiver."

The uses that are identified in advance as permissible within a zoning district are often referred to as uses "by right," which means that each use is identified as one that may be located within the district if it conforms to the design standards and other regulations that apply to the district. No specific permission is required for the use itself, only the conformance of the buildings and site features with the standards for development. Conversely, other uses may be permissible where additional standards are met to ensure that each use is compatible with the uses and character of the district. These other uses are often called "conditional uses" or "special uses." Conditional or special uses require specific approval for the use as well as approval for the development of the site.

Many situations do not exactly fit the zoning regulations, and more discretion in administration of, and decision-making about, zoning and land development situations is required. These situations provide opportunities to depart from the requirements of the zoning ordinance.

CREATING THE ABILITY TO DEPART
FROM THE ZONING REGULATIONS

For nearly nine decades, land use and development controls have been accomplished largely through zoning. Almost as long as the zoning ordinance has been the cornerstone of land use controls, there has also been a need for ways to introduce discretion and flexibility into the zoning process. Through the use of variances, conditional use permits, and special use permits, flexibility may be achieved.

Most local governments have separate bodies to render decisions about development that conforms to the land development regulations and development that departs from the zoning regulations. The planning commission or planning board is the body that renders decisions to implement the zoning ordinance, and may be the same body involved in plan making (discussed earlier). The board of adjustment is the body that renders decisions about departures from the zoning ordinance.

Some local governments separate the responsibility for creating the comprehensive plan from the responsibility for implementing the plan through approving development. This may result in three bodies:

1. A planning commission (oversees the creation, amendment, and maintenance of a comprehensive plan);

2. A development review board (implements the plan through zoning and other regulations); and

3. A board of adjustment (considers variations from the regulations).

In general, a board of adjustment is the body established to hear appeals of decisions rendered by administrators, applications for situations that depart from the zoning regulations, applications for some matters that require interpretation, and applications for matters that require the exercise of discretion. These boards have several names: "board of adjustment," "board of appeals," "board of adjustment and appeals," or "board of zoning adjustment."

The types and functions of boards of zoning adjustment vary from state to state, depending on the grant of authority provided by state-enabling legislation for planning and zoning. Case law and local practice have also influenced the types of zoning-related issues that the board may address, as well as the relationship of the board to the planning commission and the legislative body. While there are many variations among the states, there are a number of common themes.

The primary roles for boards of adjustment typically fall into three categories:

1. *A safety valve in the application of zoning regulations.* Early on, it was recognized that zoning regulations could not be written to address every circumstance of the use of property, particularly when applying zoning in developed communities. Therefore, zoning ordinances empowered the board to balance the strict application of a set

- **Chapter 8** defines the concept of due process and describes how the board ensures that the principles of due process guide them in the procedure of receiving applications, considering them, and rendering decisions.
- **Chapter 9** discusses public hearings, explains what constitutes evidence, describes the process of receiving testimony, and addresses the board's relationship with its attorney. Public hearings are at the heart of board operations.

FOR MORE INFORMATION

- The American Planning Association has an excellent website (http://www.planning.org) where you will find current information on planning, recent research results, and publications that may be of interest. Select the link to "Publications" and then to "The Commissioner." While the title refers to planning commissioners, there is information that is applicable to board members. Look at the "Jobs & Careers" link, select "Education," and then "Professional Planners" to see information for citizen planners. Check the link under "About APA," select "Chapters" and then "Chapter Websites" for links to other websites on topics of interest to your community, including guides to state statutes, training manuals, or training programs to assist citizen planners.
- The Planning Commissioners Journal website (http://www.plannersweb.com) has a wealth of information helpful to commissioners and board members.

For a closer look at zoning and the history of planning and zoning, consider the following sources:

- Babcock, Richard F. *Zoning Game: Municipal Practices and Policies.* Madison, WI: University of Wisconsin Press, 1966.
- Juergensmeyer, Julian Conrad and Thomas E. Roberts. *Land Use Planning and Development Regulation Law.* Eagan, MN: West Group, 2003.
- Krueckeberg, Donald A. *Introduction to Planning History in the United States.* New Brunswick, NJ: Center for Urban Policy Research, Rutgers, 1983.
- Smith, Herbert H. *Citizen's Guide to Zoning.* Chicago: APA Planners Press, 1983.

Many states have an agency within state government that oversees planning matters for the state and provides technical assistance to local governments. Some agencies are within the Office of the Governor; others are within a department, such as the Department of State or the Department of Commerce. Still other states have a department devoted to planning, smart growth, or growth management. Your local government staff can direct you to the appropriate website or you can search your state government website for agencies that may provide valuable information to help carry out board responsibilities.

Some states provide training and publications specifically designed to assist board of adjustment members in understanding their responsibilities and the statutory requirements to which they must adhere. Here is a sampling of helpful information:

Arizona

Arizona Department of Commerce
http://www.commerce.state.az.us/communityplanning/resource.asp
Monographs on "Common Questions," including:
- *Zoning Variances* (Issue Number 3)
- *Use Permits and Special Permits* (Issue Number 4)

New York

New York State Department of State
http://www.dos.state.ny.us
- Coon, James A. *Guide to Planning and Zoning Laws of New York State.* Local Government Technical Series. Albany: New York Department of State, 2004 (http://www.dos.state.ny.us/lgss/pdfs/planzone04.pdf).
- ____. *Guidelines for Applicants to the Zoning Board of Appeals.* Local Government Technical Series. Albany: New York Department of State, 1999 (http://www.dos.state.ny.us/lgss/pdfs/guidelns.pdf).

New York Planning Federation
http://www.nypf.org
- Willis, Harry J., David Church and James W. Hotaling. *The Short Course: A Basic Guide for Planning Boards and Zoning Boards of Appeals in NYS.* Troy, NY: New York Planning Federation, 2004 (http://www.nypf.org/publications.htm).

South Carolina

South Carolina Chapter, American Planning Association
http://www.scapa.org
- South Carolina Academy for Planning training program is provided with a specific curriculum for boards of zoning appeals,

Courses #401 *(BZA Legal Overview, Part I)* and #402 *(BZA Legal Overview, Part II)*.

Many states also provide training or publications to assist the planning commission in its responsibilities. While not designed specifically to address board of adjustment operations, there is often helpful information for board members. In particular, such information helps board members understand the planning process, and provides assistance in conducting public meetings and hearings. The following is a sample of such information:

Indiana

Indiana Planning Association
(Chapter of the American Planning Association)
http://www.indianaplanning.org/citizen_planner.html
* *Citizen Planner Training Manual.* Part 1: Plan Commission Basics (available online)

Colorado

Colorado Department of Local Affairs, Office of Smart Growth
http://www.dola.state.co.us/SmartGrowth
* *Planning Commissioners Corner* (http://www.dola.state.co.us/SmartGrowth/pccorner.htm)
* *Land Use Planning Resources* (http://www.dola.state.co.us/SmartGrowth/resources.htm) includes information on variances and links to numerous helpful websites.

Michigan

Michigan Society of Planning
(Chapter of the American Planning Association)
http://www.planningmi.org
* Publications on planning, including handbooks on tools and techniques and a list of upcoming workshops, including training for the zoning board of appeals.

New Jersey

New Jersey Planning Officials
http://www.njpo.org
* 2004 NJPO Educational Programs (http://www.njpo.org/seminars.htm)
* *The Planner* (http://www.njpo.org/planner.htm), a periodical designed for planning and zoning board members; also see the list of

upcoming training, including training for the zoning board of appeals.

North Carolina

North Carolina Chapter, American Planning Association
http://www.nc-apa.org
- *Citizen Planner Training Materials* (contains a section on zoning) (http://www.nc-apa.org/Citizen_Planner_files/ Citizen_Planner_options.htm)

Other resources include:
- The National Association of Counties (http://www.naco.org) and your state chapter of the NACO
- The National League of Cities (http://www.nlc.org) and your state league of cities
- The International City/County Management Association (http://www.icma.org), in particular the "e-Library" under "Information Resources"
- The Urban Land Institute (http://www.uli.org)

2

Partners
in Planning

In this age of NIMBY[1]-ism, it often seems that there is a never-ending supply of participants involved in the planning process. When a project is proposed that some feel is objectionable, vocal opponents crowd the meeting room. However, there is much more to participation than objection to a nearby project. The entire community development process—from the first overall plan, to implementation programs such as zoning and other regulations, and, finally, to specific development projects—has many players who should be in frequent communication. All of these players are partners in the planning process. Let's consider who they are and what they do.

THE ELECTED BODY

The elected body is the legislature for the community, which adopts ordinances and sets policy for the growth and development process. In some jurisdictions, the elected body may have the authority to delegate responsibilities (e.g., for adopting subdivision regulations). In most cases, this body adopts the zoning ordinance and other land development regulations implemented by staff, the planning commission, and the board of adjustment.

In order to be effective, there should be communication between the elected body and the other participants. In the area of variances, it often happens that a board hears and approves requests for the same type of variance several times a year. When this occurs, the board should discuss the situation with the elected body. Granting the same type of variance several times a year is a clear indication

A Variance Example

Waterfront communities often require large setbacks from the shoreline as one means of protecting the shoreline. Residents with swimming pools on these waterfront lots may want pool enclosures. The house, including the pool, is most likely situated on or near the rear setback line, so a variance is requested to accommodate the pool enclosure. The variance in this situation is likely to be relatively small, perhaps 5 feet or less into the setback. When the board routinely approves such a variance, it is a signal that a change to the setback standard should be considered. The board and the elected body should have a regular opportunity to discuss lessons learned, such as this example. This feedback loop is an important part of the overall planning and development process.

that the elected body should consider an amendment to the zoning ordinance.

Other situations routinely arise that should be part of regular meetings between the board and the elected body. For example, where the same standards are regularly applied to a type of variance (see sidebar, "A Variance Example") or to a conditional use, the elected body should also consider an amendment to the zoning ordinance to specify these standards for that use in all situations. The development can then be approved through the site plan process or other channels, rather than being the subject of an additional hearing for a conditional use or variance.

There is another advantage to elected officials and board members meeting periodically to discuss issues. Ultimately, elected officials are going to hear about unpopular board decisions regarding conditional uses or variances. It is a good idea to sit down on a regular basis to discuss hot topics, as well as to communicate with the elected body about the work that the board is doing, which can help the elected body feel a sense of confidence in the decisions that the board is making. It may not reduce the heat that elected officials are bearing, but they may better understand why they are bearing it.

Each community will have similar examples of matters that should be discussed between the elected body and the board of adjustment. Regular opportunities for communication, such as quarterly workshops or other periodic gatherings, will enhance the development process in the community.

PLANNING COMMISSION

A fundamental responsibility of a planning commission is the preparation of plans (discussed briefly in Chapter 1). In some jurisdictions, the planning commission is authorized to adopt plans and regulations. In most situations, however, the planning commission makes recommendations to the elected body about plans, plan amendments, and land development regulations.

The planning commission typically has more formal interaction with the elected body than a board of adjustment by making recommendations on matters decided by that body and through implementing the plan. Implementation may occur through development matters such as site plan review, recommendations on rezoning requests, and consideration of planned unit developments. In some jurisdictions, these implementation activities and decisions are retained by the elected body or are delegated in part to staff. Because there are so many participants in implementation, regular and meaningful communication must occur.

BOARD OF ADJUSTMENT

Through the grant of variances, waivers, or special use permits, the board of adjustment is also called upon to implement the plan. The board may encounter situations on a regular basis that should be brought to the attention of the planning commission. In the example of the variance to a shoreline setback (see sidebar, "A Variance Example"), the requirements of the zoning ordinance may be closely tied to policy articulated in the plan. Both the board and the planning commission should be part of the discussion to consider a change to the shoreline setback regulation. Such a discussion will better inform the board about the rationale for the regulation, while providing to the planning commission and the elected body the knowledge gained by the board in considering departures from the regulation.

The board of adjustment, the planning commission, and the elected body are all partners in making a great community. In order to effectively do their jobs, they must have an opportunity to share experiences, talk about lessons learned, and explore ways to achieve the results they want for their community. Periodic workshops or retreats should be held for joint discussion on topics such as goal setting, discussion of growth and development problems, review of the success or failure of programs, or current planning issues. It is important to set aside time during the year to step back, engage in long-range thinking, and affirm expectations among the different groups. The board will be more effective when the members clearly understand the expectations of the elected body that appointed them. Regular meetings between and among the groups will keep the lines of communication open and help avoid confusion or misunderstanding about roles, responsibilities, and expectations.

HEARING OFFICER OR HEARING EXAMINER

A hearing officer is an individual appointed by the local legislative or executive body to render decisions on appeals, variances, and special exceptions. The hearing officer has the same responsibilities that are otherwise assigned to a board of adjustment: conducting hearings for fact finding, applying adopted criteria to evaluate an application, reaching conclusions, and issuing written orders. As an alternative to appointing a board comprised of lay people, the use of a hearing officer allows the local government to select a person with expertise and experience in land use, zoning, and law.

SPECIAL PURPOSE BOARDS, COMMISSIONS, OR COMMITTEES

Many communities have one or several boards, commissions, or committees to deal with specific aspects of community planning and development (e.g., an historic preservation board, a community redevelopment agency, a transportation advisory board, an environmental preservation council, or an airport advisory board). Whatever the name and purpose, these groups are important in the planning process.

In some cases, the group is involved in the process of creating the plan or a closely related planning document. In other cases, the group is directly involved in development matters; some of these matters may be the subjects of requests for variances, waivers, or conditional use permits. Whatever their charge, these groups should be involved in a regularly scheduled gathering to discuss matters of planning and development with the elected body, the planning commission, and the board of adjustment.

LOCAL GOVERNMENT STAFF

Many local governments have professional planning staff, which may vary in size. It is typically the responsibility of staff to take in applications, and provide an analysis and a report on whether the requested action is consistent with the plan and complies with the regulations. A staff member attends meetings of the elected body, the planning commission, and the board of adjustment to present the report and answer questions. The staff member may be requested to make a recommendation.

Not all local governments have planning staff. In small communities, staff support for a board of adjustment may be a city clerk, a building official, or another staff person not routinely involved in planning and development. Whether a professional planner or someone else provides staff support, it is important to periodically set aside time for discussions between the board and staff, which will ensure that the board is receiving the necessary information and appropriate procedures are being followed.

If the board does not have staff available, then it may be necessary to designate a board member to act as staff for the purpose of collecting information and evaluating an application. In this case, it may be advisable for that board member not to participate in the decision-making process.

The relationship between the board and staff will be enhanced if the following principles are adopted:

• *Principle 1: Do not assume that staff can read your mind in determining what you may need and when you may need it.* For many boards, communication with staff is often limited to presentations or answering questions during hearings and meetings. Productive dialogue between board members and staff on content or outcomes may be rare. One way to improve the situation is to include time during the regular meeting for a discussion of board actions, needs, and procedures. These discussions may also be the subject of a workshop with staff.

• *Principle 2: The role of staff is to help the board be more productive.* The corollary to this principle is that staff should do what they are trained to do. For example, if staff are not currently providing an evaluation of an application, which may include a staff recommendation, this may be a place to start building a better operating relationship. Staff evaluation of an application saves the board time by defining issues and is an important part of building a record to support eventual board action. Staff have been trained to provide thorough and comprehensive evaluations, so it is advisable to use their expertise. Over time, open communication will fine tune the type, amount, and tone of the information that staff provide on each case.

- *Principle 3: The role of staff is to support and assist the board.* The board is a decision-making body. While the board may ultimately adopt findings, the board does not generate information or search out facts for consideration during a hearing. Staff should receive applications, evaluate the applications for compliance with regulations, and provide information to the board to assist in making decisions. It is important to recognize the divisions of roles and responsibilities to avoid due process and other problems (see Chapters 8 and 9).

LOCAL CITIZENS

Participation by the citizens of a community is essential to an effective planning process. This participation is not limited to the development of a plan. It is equally important that citizens have the opportunity to be heard on development matters as well. (Chapters 8 and 9 discuss due process and public hearings.) Most citizens are heard during public hearings when they appear to support—or, more often, object—to a proposed conditional use or variance.

It would be helpful to the overall planning process if the types of matters considered by the board of adjustment were discussed with citizens during general meetings about planning and development issues. These gatherings can provide an opportunity for education about board responsibilities as well as an opportunity for citizens to express their expectations and concerns for the community.

Board members want to act responsibly and in accordance with state and local law. Board members also want to be responsive, both to the general public and to the applicant. Sometimes the desire to be responsible and responsive (Figure 2-1) seems to pull the board member in two directions. Communication about development matters and expectations outside of a public hearing on an application will improve the board's ability to balance responsibility and responsiveness.

Figure 2-1. Opposing Motivations

BOARDS OF ADJUSTMENT ACROSS THE COUNTRY

All states have boards or commissions that provide the relief described and discussed in Chapters 1 and 3. However, the types and degrees of relief vary widely across the country. Some boards have responsibilities regarding conditional or special uses (discussed in Chapter 4).

Most states have specific enabling legislation to establish the board of adjustment. The legislation provides the authorization to towns, cities, counties, boroughs, and other jurisdictions for a board. These state laws also outline the roles and responsibilities that a board may assume and may address matters of membership and operation. The roles and responsibilities authorized for the board vary across the country. This section is intended to help the reader understand the range of responsibilities and to learn how individual states provide for boards of adjustment.

Board Membership

Membership typically ranges between five and seven members; however, several states allow as few as three members and some have as many as nine. Variations in membership requirements include different provisions for cities and counties, different provisions based on population or class of the city, or requirements based on geographic representation. A few states, such as Florida and Georgia, have no specific state-enabling legislation. Local governments in these states have great latitude in establishing their own requirements.

Typical variations in membership requirements include the following:

• Some states (such as Illinois, Michigan, Nebraska, Nevada, and Washington) have specific provisions for the elected body to serve as the board of adjustment.

• Board members may be elected in New Hampshire.

• Joint boards of adjustment are possible in Colorado and New Jersey.

• Several states (such as Arizona, Kansas, Nebraska, and North Carolina) provide for extraterritorial powers for the board of adjustment.

• Planning commissions may sit as the board of adjustment in Arkansas, North Carolina, South Dakota, and Vermont.

- Hearing examiners or hearing officers may be appointed to conduct hearings on special uses, conditional uses, and variances in Arizona, Idaho, and Illinois.

These examples are intended to illustrate the variety in boards across the United States. Each state has established its own provisions, many loosely modeled on *A Standard State Zoning Enabling Act*,[2] but each has its own unique requirements.

What's In a Name?

While this book uses the label "board of adjustment" throughout, many variations exist throughout the 50 states. Table 2-1 identifies the names of boards in each state. In some states, the name of a municipal board differs from the name of the county board. In other instances, more than one body is authorized to act on the matters that typically come before the board of adjustment. Specific rules are established for each instance; consult the laws in your state for the current provisions and requirements.

Roles and Responsibilities

"Special exception," "special use," and "conditional use" are terms that describe a class of land uses that may be permissible under special circumstances, as distinguished from land uses that are permissible by right. Throughout this book, the term "conditional use" is used to describe this situation.

Table 2-2 depicts the roles and responsibilities of boards of adjustment in each state and uses the terminology of that state for the "conditional use" situation. In some states, the roles and responsibilities differ between a county and a city. Counties may be authorized for one set of responsibilities and cities in the same state may be authorized for other responsibilities. In those states that have classes of cities (typically based on size), only cities in specific classes may be authorized to establish a board of adjustment. However, for purposes of Table 2-2, the broad perspective of roles within each state is provided. Refer to the specific enabling legislation for your state and local government for the details regarding what matters your board is authorized to consider in your jurisdiction.

As Table 2-2 shows, nearly every state has specific provisions to authorize boards of adjustment to grant variances. Likewise, nearly every state authorizes the board to hear appeals of administrative decisions. The majority of states have provisions for special or conditional uses.

Table 2-1. Boards of Adjustment in the 50 States

State	Board of Adjustment	Board of Appeals	Board of Adjustment and Appeals	Board of Zoning Adjustment	Board of Zoning Appeals	Zoning Board of Adjustment	Zoning Board of Appeals	Zoning Board of Review	Hearing Officer or Hearing Examiner	Planning Commission or Planning Board	Other
Alabama	✓										
Alaska										✓	
Arizona	✓								✓		
Arkansas				✓							
California				✓							Zoning Administrator
Colorado	✓										
Connecticut							✓				
Delaware	✓										
Florida											Varies locally
Georgia											Varies locally
Hawaii										✓	
Idaho											Governing body
Illinois		✓							✓		
Indiana					✓						
Iowa		✓									
Kansas					✓						
Kentucky	✓										
Louisiana	✓	✓									
Maine		✓									
Maryland		✓								✓	✓

Table 2-1. Boards of Adjustment in the 50 States (continued)

State	Board of Adjustment	Board of Appeals	Board of Adjustment and Appeals	Board of Zoning Adjustment	Board of Zoning Appeals	Zoning Board of Adjustment	Zoning Board of Appeals	Zoning Board of Review	Hearing Officer or Hearing Examiner	Planning Commission or Planning Board	Other
Massachusetts						✓					Zoning Administrator
Michigan		✓			✓						
Minnesota	✓		✓								
Mississippi				✓							
Missouri				✓							
Montana	✓										
Nebraska	✓				✓						
Nevada	✓								✓	✓	
New Hampshire	✓					✓					
New Jersey						✓				✓	
New Mexico											Zoning Authority
New York						✓					
North Carolina	✓										
North Dakota	✓										
Ohio				✓							
Oklahoma	✓										
Oregon									✓	✓	Governing Body
Pennsylvania									✓		Zoning Hearing Board
Rhode Island								✓			
South Carolina					✓						

Table 2-1. Boards of Adjustment in the 50 States (continued)

State	Board of Adjustment	Board of Appeals	Board of Adjustment and Appeals	Board of Zoning Adjustment	Board of Zoning Appeals	Zoning Board of Adjustment	Zoning Board of Appeals	Zoning Board of Review	Hearing Officer or Hearing Examiner	Planning Commission or Planning Board	Other
South Dakota	✓										
Tennessee		✓									
Texas	✓										
Utah	✓										Administrative Officer
Vermont	✓										Dev. Review Board
Virginia					✓						
Washington	✓										Zoning Adjuster
West Virginia	✓										
Wisconsin	✓										
Wyoming	✓										Governing Body

Table 2-2. Roles and Responsibilities of Boards of Adjustment

State	Special Exception	Special Use Permit	Conditional Use Permit	Variance	Appeal of Administrative Decision
Alabama	✓			✓	✓
Alaska				✓	✓
Arizona				✓	✓
Arkansas				✓	✓
California			✓	✓	✓
Colorado	✓			✓	✓
Connecticut	✓	✓		✓	✓
Delaware	✓	✓		✓	✓
Florida[a]					
Georgia[b]					
Hawaii		✓			
Idaho		✓		✓	
Illinois		✓		✓	✓
Indiana[c]	✓	✓	✓	✓	✓
Iowa	✓			✓	✓
Kansas	✓			✓	✓
Kentucky			✓	✓	✓
Louisiana[d]	✓			✓	✓
Maine[e]	✓		✓	✓	✓
Maryland	✓			✓	✓
Massachusetts		✓		✓	✓
Michigan				✓	✓
Minnesota		✓	✓	✓	✓
Mississippi		✓	✓	✓	✓
Missouri		✓		✓	✓
Montana	✓			✓	✓
Nebraska				✓	✓
Nevada[f]	✓	✓	✓	✓	✓
New Hampshire	✓			✓	✓
New Jersey			✓	✓	✓
New Mexico				✓	✓

Table 2-2. Roles and Responsibilities of Boards of Adjustment (continued)

State	Special Exception	Special Use Permit	Conditional Use Permit	Variance	Appeal of Adminis- trative Decision
New York[g]		✓		✓	✓
North Carolina	✓	✓	✓	✓	✓
North Dakota				✓	✓
Ohio			✓	✓	✓
Oklahoma	✓			✓	✓
Oregon			✓	✓	
Pennsylvania	✓		✓	✓	✓
Rhode Island		✓		✓	✓
South Carolina	✓			✓	✓
South Dakota			✓	✓	✓
Tennessee	✓			✓	✓
Texas	✓			✓	✓
Utah	✓		✓	✓	✓
Vermont				✓	✓
Virginia	✓			✓	✓
Washington			✓	✓	✓
West Virginia				✓	✓
Wisconsin	✓			✓	✓
Wyoming	✓			✓	✓

    a.   Florida does not have enabling legislation for the board of adjustment. Each local government may define roles and responsibilities.

    b.   Georgia does not have enabling legislation for the board of adjustment. Each local government may define roles and responsibilities.

    c.   Indiana board responsibilities include "contingent use."

    d.   Louisiana board responsibilities include "special exemptions" and "interpretations."

    e.   Maine board responsibilities include "interpretations."

    f.   Appeals from the Nevada board are heard by the governing body.

    g.   Variances authorized in New York include both use variances and area variances.

FOR MORE INFORMATION

State statutes provide details about board names, roles, and responsibilities. The following are the sources of information for each state.

Table 2-3. State Statutes for Boards of Adjustment

Alabama	Ala. Code §§ 11.52.80-11.52.81; Ala. Code §§ 11.19.19-11.19.20
Alaska	Alaska Stat. §§ 29.40.020-29.40.060
Arizona	Ariz. Rev. Stat. §§ 9.462.06-9.462.07; § 11.807
Arkansas	Ark. Code Ann. § 14.56.416; Ark. Code Ann. § 14.17.209
California	California Government Code § 65900-65909.5
Colorado	Colo. Rev. Stat. Ann. §§ 31.23.301; 31.23.307; Colo. Rev. Stat. Ann. §§ 30.28.117-30.28.118
Connecticut	Conn. Gen. Stat. §§ 8.3d; 8.5; 8.5a; 8.5b; 8.6; 8.6a; 8.7; 8.8; 8.9; 8.10; 8.11; 8.11a; 8.21; 8.26e; 8.28
Delaware	Del. Code Ann. tit. 22 §§ 321-332; Del. Code Ann. tit. 9 §§ 101; 1301; 1311-1314; 4913-4918; 6913-6918
Florida	No state-enabling legislation
Georgia	No state-enabling legislation
Hawaii	Haw. Rev. Stat. Ann. § 205.6
Idaho	Idaho Code §§ 67-6512; 67-6516; 67-6520
Illinois	Ill. Comp. Stat. §§ 110-35 to 55; 11-13-3; 11-13-3.1; 11-13-4; 11-13-5; 11-13-6; 11-13-7; 11-13-7a; 11-13-8 to 11-13-14; 11-13-14.1; 11-13-15 to 20; 5-12009; 5-12009.5; 5-12010 to 12019
Indiana	Ind. Code Ann. §§ 36.7.4.900-36.7.4.924; 36.7.4.1000-36.7.4.1011; 36.7.5.1.5
Iowa	Iowa Code Ann. §§ 414.7-414.18; 335.10-335.22
Kansas	Kan. Stat. Ann. §§ 12-759; 19-2962
Kentucky	Ky. Rev. Stat. Ann. §§ 100.217; 100.221; 100.223; 100.227; 100.231; 100.233; 100.237; 100.241; 100.243; 100.247; 100.251; 100.257; 100.261; 100.263
Louisiana	La. Rev. Stat. Ann. §§ 140.32; 4721; 4727
Maine	Me. Rev. Stat. Ann. tit. 30-A § 4353
Maryland	Md. Statutes § 2.08, 4.07, 8.110, 8.111, 8.112.3, 8.112.4
Massachusetts	Mass. Gen. Laws. Ann. ch. 40A §§ 9; 10; 12-16
Michigan	Mich. Comp. Laws. Ann. §§ 125.288-125.293a; 125.585; 125.585a; 125.218-125.223
Minnesota	Minn. Stat. Ann. §§ 394.26; 394.27; 394.361; 394.362; 462.357; 462.359; 462.361
Mississippi	Miss. Code Ann. § 17-1-17; Title 17 Chapter 1

Table 2-3. State Statutes for Boards of Adjustment (continued)

Missouri	Mo. Ann. Stat. §§ 65.690; 64.120; 64.281; 64.870
Montana	Mont. Code Ann. §§ 76-2-321 to 76-2-328; 76-2-221 to 76-2-228
Nebraska	Neb. Rev. Stat. §§ 15-1106; 15-1201; 15-1202; 19-907 to 19-912.01; 23-168.01 to 23-168.04
Nevada	Nev. Rev. Stat. §§ 278.270 to 278.319.5
New Hampshire	N.H. Rev. Stat. Ann. §§ 673:3; 674:33; 677:1 to 677:16; 677:19
New Jersey	N.J. Stat. Ann. §§ 40:27-6.13; 40:55D-60; 40:55D-65; 40:55D-65.1; 40:55D-70; 40:55D-70.2; 40:55D-71; 40:55D-72; 40:55D-76
New Mexico	N.M. Stat. Ann. §§ 3-19-8; 3-21-8; 3-21-9; 3-21-26
New York	NY Gen Cty § 27-b; § 38; § 81-83a
North Carolina	N.C. Gen. Stat. §§ 160A-360; 160A-362; 160A-381; 160A-388; 160A-446; 153A-340; 153A-345
North Dakota	N.D. Sent. Code §§ 40-47-01; 40-47-07 to 40-47-13; 11-33-12
Ohio	Ohio Rev. Code Ann. §§ 519.14; 519.15; 303.13; 303.14; 303.15
Oklahoma	Okla. Stat. Ann. tit. 11 §§ 44-101 to 44-110; 47-122; 19-863.1; 19-863.20; 19-863.21; 19-865.62; 19-865.63; 19-866.15; 19-866.22; 19-866.23; 19-868.18; 19-868.3; 19-869.6
Oregon	Or. Rev. Stat. §§ 197.375; 197.540; 197.805 to 197.825; 197.828 to 197.860
Pennsylvania	Pa. Stat. Ann. §§ 10901-10916.2
Rhode Island	R.I. Gen. Laws §§ 45-24-41; 45-24-42; 45-24-43; 45-24-56 to 45-24-69.1
South Carolina	S.C. Code Ann. §§ 6.29.780-6.29.860
South Dakota	S.D. Codified Laws §§ 11.4.13-11.4.28; §§ 11.2.49-11.2.63
Tennessee	Tenn. Code Ann. §§ 13-7-205 to 13-7-207; 13-7-106 to 13-7-109
Texas	Tex. Code Ann. §§ 211.008-211.011; 231.018-231.021
Utah	Utah Code Ann. §§ 10-9-701 to 10-9-708; 17-27-701 to 17-27-708
Vermont	Vt. Stat. Ann. tit. 24 §§ 4461-4470; 1012
Virginia	Va. Code Ann. §§ 15.2-2203; 15.2-2308 to 15.2-2314
Washington	Wash. Rev. Code. Ann. §§ 35A.63.110; 36.70.200 to 36.70.310; 36.70.810 to 36.70.900
West Virginia	W. Va. Code §§ 19-12A-11
Wisconsin	Wis. Stat. Ann. §§ 60.65; 59.693(4)(b); 59.694; 59.696; 59.697
Wyoming	Wyo. Stat. Ann. §§ 15.1.601-15.1.611; Wyo. Stat. Ann. § 18.5.106

Notes

1. An acronym for "Not in My Backyard," which refers to the situation where people object to a use or development that they feel should be located elsewhere.

2. U.S. Department of Commerce, Advisory Committee on Zoning. *A Standard State Zoning Enabling Act.* Washington, DC: U.S. Government Printing Office, 1922.

PART

II

Zoning Matters

3

Relief Valves in Zoning

Through the zoning ordinance, land within a jurisdiction is divided into districts or zones. Within each zone, specified uses may be established. The standards that govern such matters as building location, building dimensions, placement and quantity of parking, landscaping, and other features included in "site design" are uniform within the district, but may vary from one district to another. While the intent is to achieve some uniformity of use and site design within a district, the land that exists within the district is not uniform. Lots and parcels of land vary in topography with features such as bodies of water, outcroppings of rock, sinkholes, or 100-year old trees.

VARIANCES

In recognition of this fact, most zoning ordinances provide an opportunity for a property owner to request permission to vary from the requirements of a zoning ordinance, which is called a "variance."

There are two types of variances: "use variances" and "site design variances." A use variance is a method by which a property owner is granted permission to use his property in a manner that is not currently authorized by the zoning ordinance. A site design variance is a method by which a property owner is granted permission to vary from the dimensional requirements that apply to his property. Thus, the use variance pertains solely to how the property is utilized, while the site design variance pertains solely to how an authorized use is designed.

Use Variances

As a general rule, most local governments do not allow a board to grant use variances. Thus, unless state law establishes authority for a use variance, a board should not grant a variance that allows a use not otherwise permissible in the zoning district. The basis for this prohibition is that the approval of a use variance could be considered to constitute a rezoning, which is not an action that is within the board's scope of authority. Indeed, the granting of a use variance could be considered to be a usurpation of the elected body's power.

If an elected body desires to establish the possibility of allowing uses not permissible by right, the means to do so is through a conditional or special use (discussed in Chapter 4).

Site Design Variances

The crux of a request for a site design variance is the existence of physical features that are unique to a particular parcel or lot that preclude an owner from using his property in a manner similar to other properties within the same zoning district.

Most states have included in the enabling legislation several requirements that should be met before a board grants a variance. While not all of these requirements apply in every state, the following are the typical rules applicable to the grant of a variance.

• *Rule 1: Special circumstances apply to the property.* Some states define specific circumstances, such as topography and the shape of a lot. Other states have a broad range of circumstances that may be considered special. Typically, special circumstances mean irregularity in the shape of the lot, exceptional topographical features, or other physical conditions. Some jurisdictions may identify historic or specimen trees, wetlands, bodies of water, geologic features, roads with a tree canopy, archaeological features, nesting sites, and protected views as circumstances that may require a variance in order to achieve protection.

Typical requirements in the enabling legislation may read as follows:

> Because of special circumstances applicable to the property, including its site, shape, location, or surroundings, the strict application of the zoning ordinance will deprive such property of privileges enjoyed by other property of the same classification in the same zoning district.

Another way to word this same provision is as follows:

Due to peculiar conditions, a strict interpretation of the zoning ordinance would result in an unnecessary hardship.

The idea is that the lot existed with specific physical conditions prior to the imposition of the zoning requirements. The provisions of the zoning ordinance may be appropriate for most lots within the district but limit the development of the affected lot to the point of hardship. These physical conditions are present in such a location or in such quantity that the property cannot be developed in compliance with district standards. Furthermore, the features themselves may have value to the community, and the variation in site design standards is a trade-off in achieving protection of the features.

The property owner is entitled to reasonable use of her property. The jurisdiction is entitled to protection of valued features and to development that complies with local ordinances. The variance may be the means to balance these potentially conflicting entitlements.

However, many variances are not the result of such noble purposes. Often, the property owner wishes to achieve a particular design and is unable to do so because of some physical conditions of the property. Alternate designs are possible but do not meet the property owner's preferences or may not yield the best economic return. It is inappropriate to grant such variances.

• *Rule 2: Special circumstances render the property undevelopable.* A property owner is not entitled to a variance simply because he cannot obtain the maximum economic return from his property. Rather, the board should only grant a variance when a physical feature of the property (e.g., a steep slope or an irregular lot configuration), coupled with the local government's regulations, preclude the property owner from obtaining reasonable use of his property. The burden is on the property owner to demonstrate that, without a variance, the physical feature precludes reasonable use of the property.

• *Rule 3: The applicant did not create the hardship.* A typical provision is that the situation creating the need for a variance cannot be self-created. The premise here is that the property owner did not take action to modify the lot or parcel with the result that it no longer has any reasonable use.

What actions could result in the loss of reasonable use? A typical situation is dividing a parcel that can be developed in compliance with the regulations into two lots, resulting in one lot that is too small in area or dimensions to meet the zoning regulations. In an area with significant wetlands, a property owner might divide a parcel to create a good lot and a lot with most of the wetlands on it. A common situation in waterfront communities is to build a house in compliance with the regulations, leaving the addition of a pool or pool enclosure to a later date and a separate action. Once the house is built, with too little room remaining for the pool or pool enclosure to meet shoreline setbacks, a hardship exists. What is the hardship? Most lots in the neighborhood have pools with enclosures. How did the hardship arise? Lack of forethought in siting the house created the situation.

By adopting a standard that the applicant did not create the hardship, the local jurisdiction is trying to avoid a deliberate bypassing of zoning regulations through a piecemeal approach to development. Because a variance grants permission to develop land without complying with all of the zoning regulations, it is important to ensure that the variance is justified by something other than the applicant's previous actions.

A common result of some of the actions described above is the creation of a substandard lot, which is then sold to another person. The buyer does not know the lot is substandard until he attempts to develop it. The new property owner did not create the hardship, but the end result is the same. Many communities address this situation with a requirement that every lot be platted. Through the approval of a plat—even a two-lot plat—the local government can ensure that all lots created through land division are able to comply with the zoning regulations.

• *Rule 4: The variance will not alter the character of the neighborhood.* This provision is intended to protect the compatibility of the neighborhood. At the core of the variance request is the need to be treated differently with regard to the zoning regulations; however, this different treatment may result in an incompatibility within the neighborhood. What factors should be considered? The board should consider the factors of compatibility for conditional uses (described in Chapter 4).

The use that receives a variance should fit the neighborhood in terms of scale, site features, intensity of development, and other design aspects. The principles of compatibility do not require sameness. The principles of compatibility do require harmony and transition from one use to another. The board has the responsibility to consider the factors of compatibility and attach conditions to the grant of a variance to ensure that the use will not negatively impact the neighborhood to the point that the neighborhood's character is changed.

It is important in considering neighborhood character to remember that the variance is intended to restore equity to the property owner, but not to grant an advantage to the property owner. The need for the variance arose from a physical condition of the property. The variance should modify the zoning regulations enough to make development and reasonable use possible, but not so much as to grant special privilege to the property owner. When evaluating whether the variance will alter the character of the neighborhood, consider that the purpose of the variance is to bring this property up to the level of similarly located and zoned properties, and nothing more. This leads to the next rule of variances.

• *Rule 5: A variance should be the minimum that will afford relief.* When it has been demonstrated that special circumstances exist, that the special circumstances meet the standards set by the local jurisdiction and result in a hardship, and that the applicant did not create the hardship, the board must consider the extent of the variance. This is closely related to the rule that the variance should not alter the character of the neighborhood (see Rule 4, above). By granting only the minimum variation in the regulations that will grant relief to the property owner, the board can better address the compatibility needs of the neighborhood.

This rule helps ensure that the granting of a variance does not confer special privileges on the property owner that are not enjoyed by other similarly situated properties. This rule also eliminates the grant of a variance for social or personal hardships, which are not a proper basis for hardship in any case.

The board should take care to review each application on its own merit. Previous decisions—especially those that were not made in accordance with the rules governing variances—do not set a precedent. Poorly supported decisions in the past should not lead to poor decisions now or in the future.

• *Rule 6: Conditions may be assigned to meet the purpose of the variance regulations.* The board has a responsibility to ensure that all state and local requirements are met before a variance is granted. Often these requirements provide some latitude in the decision rendered by the board, including the ability to attach conditions. These conditions should be the requirements that ensure compatibility, that the property owner does not receive special privileges, and that the variance is the minimum modification necessary to achieve the purpose. The conditions should be consistent with the spirit and intent of the zoning regulations, and should be designed to minimize any adverse impact that may arise from the grant of a variance.

If the state legislation and local elected body wish to establish the possibility of allowing uses not permissible by right, the means to do so is through the conditional or special use (see Chapter 4). The grant of a use variance is generally not an appropriate means to allow a use otherwise not permissible in the zoning district.

Board's Analysis of Requests for Site Design Variances

In summary, a board should not grant a variance unless the board has determined that each of the following criteria exist:

1. Special circumstances apply to the property;
2. Special circumstances render the property undevelopable;
3. The applicant did not create the hardship;
4. The variance will not alter the character of the neighborhood; and
5. The variance is the minimum that will afford relief.

Moreover, even if all of these criteria exist, the board has the authority and duty to impose reasonable conditions to ensure that the granting of the variance will not adversely affect the surrounding properties.

INTERPRETATIONS

A zoning ordinance is sometimes unclear on some particular point, or a regulation may be stated in two parts of the ordinance in different ways. In this case, the ordinance must be interpreted. To interpret the ordinance means to determine the exact meaning of a provision, or to determine how a provision should be applied.

Some jurisdictions assign the responsibility for these interpretations to a staff person, such as the zoning administrator, a department director, or another senior- or executive-level person. However, it is also fairly common to assign the responsibility for interpretation to the board of adjustment.

How are interpretations made? One important factor is consistency. The jurisdiction should keep a written record of interpretations. It is a good idea to use interpretations to formulate amendments to the zoning ordinance. Rather than continuing to interpret the same provision repeatedly, the board can recommend to the elected body that the zoning ordinance be revised to restate the provision consistent with the interpretation.

To interpret a provision is to explain what it means. The board should not only read the provision itself, but should also read any intent statements in the zoning ordinance. When the elected body has stated a purpose or intent for the provisions within the ordinance or a section of the ordinance, it is an important guide to how the provision should be read. Consultation with the board's attorney or the local government's attorney is especially helpful as there are legal principles to guide the board in making an interpretation.

Interpreting the Map

Another type of interpretation is the interpretation of the zoning map. Some zoning maps are at a scale where it is hard to distinguish the location of a small parcel and determine which zoning district applies. Again, the responsibility for interpreting the map may be assigned to the board of adjustment. Many jurisdictions have rules for map interpretation, guidelines for determining boundary lines, and the subsequent determination of which zoning district applies.

It is a good idea to adopt rules for interpretation. These rules state whether a boundary line follows the centerline or right-of-way line on a road, for example. As with the interpretation of written provisions in the zoning regulations, it is a good practice to keep a record of interpretations. The record of past interpretations serves as a guide to future interpretations. It also assists in the revision of the zoning map by incorporating the details of interpretations on the map.

APPEALS OF ADMINISTRATIVE DECISIONS

In jurisdictions that delegate some level of final authority to staff, it is typical for the local government's regulations to authorize an appeal of such decisions to the board. A local government may also allow a party to challenge an interpretation by staff of the local government's land use regulations. Because staff makes the decision rather than the elected body or the planning commission, staff's decision is referred to as an "administrative decision"; a challenge to staff's decision is called an "administrative appeal."

Unless otherwise set forth in the local government's regulations, the party challenging staff's decision has the burden of demonstrating that staff's decision or interpretation is incorrect. It is also typical that the board be required to provide great deference to staff when it has rendered interpretations of the local government's land use regulations. If staff's interpretation is reasonable, it should be upheld. Only when a party has demonstrated that staff's interpretation is unreasonable should the board overturn staff's interpretation. This standard is typically referred to as the "fairly debatable standard" (i.e., staff's interpretation must be upheld if it is fairly debatable that staff's interpretation is correct).

4

One Size Does Not Fit All: Conditional and Special Uses

Certain unusual land uses may require special controls; even common land uses may require special controls in some zoning districts. A land use that is identified in advance as permissible within a zoning district is often referred to as a "by-right" use. This land use may be located in the district if it conforms to the standards and criteria of the land development regulations. Approval may be granted by staff, by the planning commission, by a development review board, or some other body, so long as the proposed development is shown to meet the requirements of the regulations.

On the other hand, additional standards may be needed for specific uses to ensure that they are compatible with the character of the neighborhood or district. The terminology varies from state to state and among local governments within a state. These "other" uses are typically called "conditional uses," "special uses," or "special exceptions." These uses are reviewed by the board of adjustment, which assigns conditions to the approval in order to ensure compatibility.

CONDITIONAL AND SPECIAL USES

The difference between conditional uses, special uses, and special exceptions is primarily one of terminology. Throughout the country, zoning ordinances contain provisions to allow use or development only after an additional review process and assignment of conditions to the approval. Typical labels for this situation are "conditional

The Need for Conditions

It has long been established that it is desirable to have certain nonresidential uses within residential neighborhoods. Schools, churches, parks and playgrounds, day care centers, and neighborhood shops are all nice to have within walking distance or a short drive from the neighborhood. However, in order to allow such uses, the community wants to be able to assign conditions to limit impacts and ensure that a given use will be compatible.

Likewise, an industrial area is expected to have a range of manufacturing, assembly, warehousing, or distribution uses. However, the district may benefit from such commercial uses as day care centers, restaurants, or branch banks close to the work place. Again, the community wants to ensure compatibility and limit negative impacts from uses. A day care center in an industrial area requires careful attention to safety factors because the characteristics of industrial development (truck traffic, for example) are very different from the characteristics of day care centers. Likewise, parks in residential neighborhoods may have play fields that have lights and impact nearby homes.

To ensure that appropriate standards are applied, the ordinance should address the types of conditions that may be applied. The more guidance provided in the zoning ordinance, the better.

Identifying Impacts

What are the impacts of a given use? Consider the recreation center. One proposed recreation center might have only indoor facilities, such as game rooms, exercise rooms, a gym, or space for classes and programs. Another recreation center may have all of these indoor activities as well as ball fields, outdoor courts, playgrounds, or swimming pools. The amount of parking required will vary widely as well as the need for outdoor lighting, loudspeakers, and other features with negative impacts. Through the review of a recreation center as a conditional use, impacts can be identified and appropriate standards applied as a condition of approval.

use," "conditional use permit," "use on review," "special use," "special use permit," "special permit," "special exception," and "conditional zoning certificate." All such uses are called "conditional" uses in the remainder of this chapter.

There is an underlying—and often unspoken—belief that by-right uses identified as permitted within a zoning district are similar in type and in range of impacts. To some degree, the potential impacts of by-right uses are controlled through the imposition of dimensional standards. The result is a similarity of building location, orientation, and height. Other site design requirements ensure similar landscaping, driveway locations, and limits on accessory structures.

Conditional uses are likely to have greater impacts, even if the same site design requirements are imposed for the principal building and accessory structures. The ability to assign additional or different site design standards as a condition of approval makes it possible to consider uses that may provide desirable services but may create undesirable impacts.

A community may implement conditional uses for several reasons:

• The conditional use is not typical for the zoning district and the categories of uses associated with the district. However, there is a belief that the conditional use can fit the zoning district if additional requirements are applied.

• There is an expectation that the conditional use may have impacts beyond those anticipated for the zoning district.

• The local government is unable to fully anticipate the impacts that may be associated with the conditional use. It is often impossible to anticipate the type, intensity, and impact of activities that may be part of the conditional use. In a conditional use review, activities are defined, impacts are identified, and conditions are set to ensure that the use fits the neighborhood.

• The conditional use may be desirable within the district, but may require additional development standards in order to ensure compatibility.

Additional standards are needed in order to ensure that the conditional use meets these requirements:

• It will be compatible or in harmony with the area in which it is located;

• It will not endanger public health or safety;

• It will be appropriate in the specific location where it is proposed; and

- It will be designed in such a way as to mitigate potential conflicts with adjacent and nearby uses.

Some zoning ordinances have lists of permitted and prohibited
uses, and further specify that any use that is not identified as permitted or prohibited is potentially allowable as a conditional use. This is
problematic for several reasons. There are no guidelines as to what
uses may be appropriate in a particular zoning district. In the absence
of an extensive list of permitted and prohibited uses, many inappropriate uses may be proposed. In the absence of guidelines on the
assignment of conditions, the conditions may be inadequate to ensure
compatibility. Development occurs through an unending series of
negotiations, interpretations, and, too often, litigation. It is much better to specify the uses that may be allowable subject to conditions and
provide clear guidelines for the assignment of conditions.

What are "Conditions"?

The term "conditions" is used because the approval is subject to
additional design standards or is subject to compliance with different
or additional standards. These additional requirements are the conditions under which approval is granted. This means that the development must meet standards that apply to the zoning district plus
those standards that are imposed as conditions of approval. Therefore, the development and use of the site is limited by the additional
requirements. The conditions of approval have the same weight and
importance as the standards and criteria that are specified in the land
development regulations for the by-right uses. Often, the approval is
identified with one of the following labels: "conditional use permit,"
"special use permit," or "special exception." Regardless of the label,
the reasons for assigning conditions are centered on the concept of
compatibility.

General and Specific Conditions

The flexibility and discretion inherent in the ability to assign conditions to certain use approvals can also lead to significant problems.
The zoning ordinance should contain standards to guide the assignment of conditions. Very detailed standards, similar to the dimensional standards for the permitted uses, limit the flexibility inherent
in the conditional use approval process. However, where the standard is broad and general (such as "must not be detrimental to the
health, safety, or welfare of the surrounding area"), negotiations will
take place between the property owner and the board on how to

meet the standard. Such an overly generalized standard is suscepti-
ble to legal challenge as resulting conditions may be arbitrary.

As an important part of periodic workshops and conversations
between the board and the planning commission, the level of detail
issue in conditional use standards should be a priority. It is important to strike a balance between standards that are too broad and
standards that are so narrowly drawn as to remove the ability to
assign conditions to ensure compatibility.

A good model for conditional uses is found in the *Growing Smart
Legislative Guidebook,*[1] which recommends that conditions be adopted
that "promote the intent and purpose of the local comprehensive
plan and land development regulations." The list should include
conditions that:

(a) "minimize the adverse effect of a development on the surrounding area and on any natural resources that will be affected by
the development;

(b) require the submission and approval of a site plan, if authorized by the land development regulations, that specifies the location
and nature of the development and any necessary improvements;

(c) guarantee the satisfactory completion and maintenance of any
required improvements;

(d) control the sequence of development, including when it must
be commenced and completed; and

(e) require detailed records, including drawings, maps, plats, or
specifications."[2]

CONCEPTS OF COMPATIBILITY

An essential ingredient in the planning and design of cities and neighborhoods is the relationship of buildings to neighboring buildings
and streets, such that all of the parts add up to a coherent and balanced whole. "Compatibility" is the term used to describe this relationship; however, the question of how to define the relationship
plagues local government officials. As a planning principle, this term
is used to describe the situation where adjacent and nearby buildings,
activities, and land uses fit together in a way to achieve balance and
harmony in the neighborhood. The degree of "fit" is based on the
presence, absence, or mitigation of impacts from the new use or building to existing uses or buildings in the neighborhood.

This means that different uses can exist in the same neighborhood
and can be adjacent to each other over a period of time without creating an unacceptable degree of negative impacts, which is called "sta-

bility." Stability means that a community, neighborhood, or place has balance and endures as a place with consistent character. "Instability" means unreasonable and unplanned change, a loss of identity, and a loss of the sense of place and comfort people want in their neighborhoods. Compatibility does not mean absolute sameness nor lack of change, but it does mean that new uses fit the neighborhood and that the degree of change or difference is not so great as to create excessive or inordinate impacts. Because neighborhood stability is an essential component of compatibility, compatibility is measured in terms of how well a use will fit into the neighborhood where it is proposed.

Impacts of Development

"Impact" describes the effect of one use on another. It is the effect of some man-made action that alters the character of a land use, neighborhood, or community due to the introduction of a new land use or building. This new use or building interferes with the expected use or activity within the neighborhood or community.

An impact can be either positive or negative. Positive impacts result in a change for the better (e.g., improved air quality, improved water quality, or other improvements to quality of life). Negative impacts, often labeled as incompatibility, result in a change to a worse situation.

Consider the following negative impacts that may arise from a proposed new use or development:

- *Traffic impacts:* increased congestion, reduced safety, reduced efficiency, and increased noise
- *Visual impacts:* loss of important views or a less pleasing appearance of buildings and landscapes
- *Environmental impacts:* significant change in air, water, or land resources (e.g., increased pollution, loss of important habitats, or loss of important features such as wetlands)
- *Nuisance impacts:* increased noise, lights from vehicles, exterior lights in parking lots or around buildings, odor, or vibration
- *Privacy impacts:* encroachment of tall buildings, outdoor gathering places (e.g., recreation facilities), or increased density or intensity of development
- *Safety and welfare impacts:* decreased safety and reduced protection from hazards (e.g., fire, explosion, or flooding)

Some impacts are more readily defined and regulated than others. Typically, a zoning ordinance includes use and site design standards, along with other development regulations based on the impacts asso-

What is a Neighborhood?

A "neighborhood" is defined as a group of people, homes, and supporting uses related to each other, whose relationship may be defined by a civic facility; gathering space; or by social, political, or economic interactions. Neighborhoods are often defined by specific boundaries or physical features.

The definition of a neighborhood is somewhat variable in the planning literature, but is most often focused on an objective measure of size (up to 5,000 population) or level of interaction in an area with characteristics that distinguish it from other areas, sometimes with boundaries defined by physical barriers or natural features.[1] Others have described the neighborhood as being most clearly defined when social and physical spaces coincide.[2]

It is important to the evaluation of a proposed conditional use to specify the area of impact. One of the most common techniques in zoning ordinances is to describe a specific distance from the proposed project (e.g., 300, 500, or 1,000 feet). This is convenient because it is easily measured. It may also coincide with the area where mailed notice is required. It is uniform from one project to another.

On the other hand, the distance is not likely to relate to the actual area of the neighborhood. Furthermore, impacts may occur well beyond the specified distance. The practical effect of evaluating impact within a specified distance is to focus on a portion of the neighborhood, when the impacts affect the entire neighborhood and possibly beyond.

When no distance requirement is provided to define the neighborhood for purposes of evaluating a proposed conditional use, there will often be a dispute over the area to be included for the evaluation. However, there is an advantage in not specifying a distance. The neighborhood may be more accurately defined, based on a definition of neighborhood. It is a mistake to avoid the situation. Either define the term "neighborhood" or establish a distance from the proposed use to encompass the area of impact.

---

1. DeChiara, Joseph and Lee Koppelman. *Urban Planning and Design Criteria.* New York: Van Nostrand Reinhold Co., 1975.
2. Rapoport, Amos. *Human Aspects of Urban Form.* New York: Pergamon Press, 1977.

ciated with the by-right uses. The design standards typically include limitations of building height, requirements for building separation, and requirements to provide landscaping or landscaped buffers.

When conditional uses are evaluated, the categories of impacts may be fairly well known but the actual impacts are not so easily anticipated. Impacts from noise and lights may be anticipated and regulated through standards for location of site features, shielding of lights, or requirements for buffers. Anticipated impacts from traffic may be more easily quantified and regulated through requirements for concurrency, limitations on trip generation, or requirements for installation of transportation improvements.

However, other impacts are less readily quantified and regulated, such as perceptions of crowding, a sense of comfort and privacy, the continuity of design features throughout a neighborhood, a change in the character of the neighborhood, and stability of the neighborhood. All of the potential impacts are important in determining the compatibility of the proposed use and development of land.

PRINCIPLES OF COMPATIBILITY

Many planners agree that design is inherent in all regulations, whether explicit or hidden. The total effect of each aspect of regulation is the design of a project, which determines whether it will be considered compatible. This is an important point. Compatibility is not a beauty contest. There are specific factors of compatibility that can be measured and evaluated. These are the factors that should be identified and addressed in approving conditional uses.

The following principles are useful in guiding the assignment of conditions:

• *Principle 1: Compatible uses do not overwhelm other uses.* How can a use overwhelm its neighbors? A use would be considered overwhelming when its size or scale (e.g., height, bulk, and mass) is significantly greater than its neighbors. A high-rise building in a low-rise neighborhood will overwhelm the immediately adjacent buildings as well as the entire neighborhood. Large expanses of single- or two-story buildings with long walls unbroken by windows or doors also create an imposing neighborhood presence, as do the acres of paved parking needed to support them. The overall size of the new building may create a sense of overcrowding, even where the proposed building does not exceed density or intensity limits.

• *Principle 2: Compatible uses do not intrude into the neighborhood.* A new building may create a loss of privacy due to the height of the building relative to the surrounding buildings. Windows, balconies, or exterior hallways may provide a direct and often close view into adjacent buildings and yards. Intrusion may also take the form of blocked views, excess shadowing, or distinct differences in building style, color, or materials.

• *Principle 3: Compatible uses have appropriate site design features.* Traditional setbacks and buffers, even with fences or walls, may be useless to achieve compatibility among uses that are significantly different in intensity, scale, height, and bulk. The placement of accessory structures—especially dumpsters, loudspeakers, and security lights—may have significant impacts on adjacent uses and the entire neighborhood. Driveways, parking lots, and outdoor gathering spaces are all site design features that have great potential for negative impacts.

• *Principle 4: Compatible uses have appropriate transitions from nearby uses.* "Transition" is a familiar concept when used to describe the gradual decrease in density and intensity of land use districts from an activity center outward. However, transition in site design features (e.g., building height, residential density, or lot size) may contribute significantly to achieving compatibility.

• *Principle 5: Compatible uses contribute to stable neighborhoods.* Cities and neighborhoods change over time. Unplanned and unwelcome change creates instability. Stable neighborhoods slowly change, if at all, over a period of time, but the change should not be forced through the introduction of incompatible uses.

ASSIGNING CONDITIONS

The conditions that are required for approval of a proposed conditional use should be consistent with the principles of compatibility.

Building Heights and Dimensions

The scale and proportion of new development should be compatible with the neighborhood. The goal may be the preservation of the existing appearance of the area. In this case, conditions will prohibit excessive differences in building size, style, and materials. Where diversity is acceptable, compatibility will be achieved when limits are established on the degree of difference between the proposed buildings and the existing neighborhood.

This does not mean that the new building cannot be taller than any existing building; however, a new building must fit in. A condition to limit height will ensure that the new building does not overwhelm

Figure 4-1. Transition of Building Heights

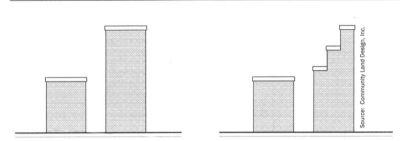

Source: Community Land Design, Inc.

The scaled steps in the building on the right create transition from a smaller building to a taller building.

its neighbors. How tall is too tall? This will depend in part on the degree of separation between buildings. The closer the buildings are to each other, the greater the negative impact from the taller building. As separation increases, taller buildings may be possible without significant negative impact and the use of landscaped buffers between buildings becomes more effective. However, the distance required to achieve effective buffering may be very large for high-rise buildings.

Even in situations where buildings are not too tall for their surroundings, they may not fit well because of the vast expanse—the length and width—of the building. This is particularly true when the building has long, blank walls with few or no doors and windows. Another way to address this situation is through the requirement of exterior features that create similarity with the surrounding neighborhood, in terms of door and window placement and building style.

It may be appropriate to establish a maximum amount of deviation from the average height and dimensions of buildings in the surrounding area. For example, an increase in height of 1.5 times the height of nearby buildings would be considered compatible and would be an appropriate condition. The condition could require that increases in height only occur in steps. This stepwise increase in building height will ensure transition between tall and short buildings.

Another aspect of building height is the relationship of the building to the street. This is based on the ratio between the width of the street corridor and the height of the walls of that corridor, which are the buildings along the street. A pleasing or satisfying ratio exists where the height of the building is approximately three times the

Compatibility Provisions in
Okaloosa County, Florida

The following draft provisions from Okaloosa County, Florida, illustrate the concept of achieving compatibility through transition in scale and site design features.

A proposed development shall be considered compatible if it meets all of the following criteria:

(1) The lot arrangement, including width, depth, and area, shall be consistent with the average width, depth, and area for the neighborhood. Variations are allowable; however, each dimension shall not vary from the average width, depth, or area by more than twenty percent more or less than the average.

(2) The type or style of buildings is generally consistent with the predominant building type or style in the neighborhood. Where an existing neighborhood exhibits considerable variety in types and styles of buildings, there is a wider variety of potentially allowable building types and styles.

(3) Building mass, scale, height, and orientation shall be consistent with the mass, scale, height, and orientation of buildings in the surrounding neighborhood. Variations are allowable: building mass shall not exceed the typical building mass by more than 150%; building heights shall not exceed average building heights by more than 150%.

(4) Building setbacks should not vary from the average building setback in the surrounding neighborhood by more than 10 percent more or less than the average building setback.

(5) The location, design, and extent of parking shall be consistent with the typical parking lot design in the surrounding neighborhood.

(6) Delivery and loading areas, dumpsters, and mechanical equipment should be located away from property lines abutting residential areas.

width of the street (a 3:1 ratio).[3] This is especially important in traditional urban neighborhoods.

Building Setbacks

A "setback" is the distance from the property line to the building. In situations where a proposed building has larger dimensions or height than buildings in the surrounding area, a condition to increase the building setback is appropriate. A greater setback provides additional open space and separation between the proposed building and adjacent buildings. An increased setback serves to mitigate the impact of buildings with greater bulk, reduce the perception of crowding, and mitigate the possible loss of privacy.

In situations where larger setbacks are not required to mitigate the impacts from large buildings, the setback should be similar to the surrounding neighborhood. This may be achieved by requiring setbacks to conform to those established in the land development regulations. As an alternative, the setbacks could conform to the average setbacks in the surrounding area, with or without a specified degree of difference.

Building Orientation

The relationship of entrances (typically in the front) and delivery or loading areas (typically in the back) to the street and to other buildings is called the "building orientation." Potential impacts may arise from anticipated noise at the main entrance as well as at delivery or loading areas.

Uses with late hours of operations or large numbers of customers may create noise from the gathering of people as they enter and leave the building or grounds. The side or rear of a building is the typical location for deliveries and trash collection. In order to assign effective conditions, it is important to evaluate the relationship between these features of a proposed use and nearby uses, especially residential uses. Changing the locations of these features through changing the orientation of the building is one condition that can serve to mitigate the impacts from noise of operations, deliveries, and gatherings of people.

Site Features

Every site has numerous features that may cause negative impacts. The features that may be of concern include parking lots, parking lot lighting, security lighting, outdoor storage, storage buildings, fences,

Figure 4-2. Building Location as a Buffering Technique

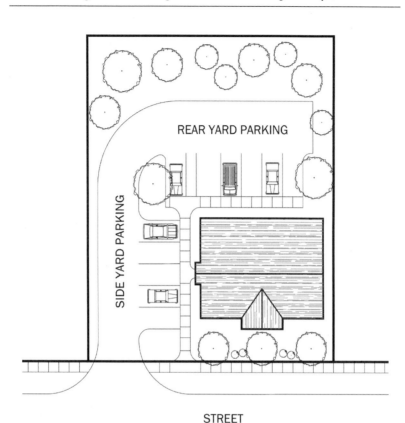

REAR YARD PARKING

SIDE YARD PARKING

STREET

Source: Community Land Design, Inc.

The parking lot on the side is separated from uses to the right of the building by the building itself.

signs, outdoor sales areas, drive-up windows, and dumpsters. Negative impacts associated with these features typically include appearance, noise, lights, and odors.

Appearance may include building materials, roof pitch, color, or architectural style. Conditions needed to ensure a good fit into the surrounding area include requiring similarity in building materials or color to the predominant theme of the area. In a neighborhood of pitched roofs, a flat roof would be inappropriate; a condition may require a pitched roof in keeping with the neighborhood. Especially

Figure 4-3. Landscaped Buffer

| COMMERCIAL SITE | LANDSCAPE BUFFER WITH BERM | RESIDENTIAL SITE |

Effective use of both a berm and landscaping ensures compatibility.

in historic districts or districts with an established architectural style, conditions may address architectural features and style to ensure that the proposed building fits with its neighbors.

Noise impacts typically come from use of the parking lot or from trucks in the delivery area engaged in loading and unloading. Placement of loudspeakers associated with drive-up windows may be a significant factor in noise. Conditions to mitigate these impacts include the location and design of the parking lot, delivery area, or drive-up window. It may be necessary to require noise abatement techniques. Separating a noise-producing feature from nearby uses can be accomplished through large setbacks; placing the building between nearby uses and the source of the noise; or using fences, walls, or berms to reduce the noise.

Lighting impacts are due to outdoor lights in parking lots and pedestrian areas, as well as lighted signs and security lighting on the building. Light may spill over to adjacent properties. Conditions may be assigned to mitigate the impacts of lighting, such as limiting the height of light poles, requiring shielding, requiring directional lighting, reducing the number of lights, or limiting the intensity of lighting.

Odors are typically associated with some manufacturing processes, but most often are connected to dumpster placement, particularly for restaurants. Conditions requiring placement of a dumpster away from nearby buildings, and possible enclosure of the dumpster, can serve to mitigate these impacts.

Other conditions that may be imposed include:

- Limiting the hours of operation;
- Specifying location and design for outdoor sales and storage;

- Designating specific locations for driveways;
- Establishing standards for the location and design of landscaping and landscaped buffers; and
- Defining standards for the location and design of fences and walls.

Limiting the hours of operation serves to reduce noise from gatherings of people and limits the time that parking lots are in use. Along with limiting hours of operation, it may be necessary to limit hours when truck deliveries may occur. Outdoor sales areas may be located away from nearby uses to reduce noise and impacts from traffic; such areas may also be limited in hours of operation to reduce impacts. The location of driveways away from adjacent buildings and uses mitigates the impact of vehicle noise. Landscaping—in particular, landscaped buffers—serves to mitigate impacts of appearance, lights, and, to some degree, noise. When combined with a berm, landscaped buffers serve to provide an attractive separation of proposed uses from existing uses.

FOR MORE INFORMATION

- The APA Store at the American Planning Association website (http://www.planning.org/store) is an excellent place to find books and reports that address conditional uses, special uses, and compatibility. In particular, consider *Practice of Local Government Planning*, by Linda C. Dalton, Charles Hoch, and Frank S. So (Washington, DC: International City/County Management Association, 2000). This book contains a wide range of information on making and implementing plans.

- *Preparing a Conventional Zoning Ordinance* (Planning Advisory Service Report Number 460) by Charles A. Lerable (Chicago: APA Planning Advisory Service, 1995) provides helpful information on exceptions, a comparison of permitted uses and conditional uses, and a list of sources of additional information in the appendix.

- *Lehman's Zoning Trilogy* (Lehman & Associates) is available through the APA Planners Book Service (http://www.planning.org/bookservice). This three-volume set has an extensive dictionary, model zoning language, and a book of zoning diagrams.

Several states have model zoning ordinances or model land development regulations. Here are some of the models available to provide additional help on regulating conditional and special uses:

- The American Law Institute (http://www.ali.org)

- Florida Department of Community Affairs (http://www.dca.state.fl.us)
- Georgia Department of Community Affairs (http://www.dca.state.ga.us)
- State of Washington Department of Community, Trade and Economic Development (http://www.ocd.wa.gov/growth)

Notes

1.   Meck, Stuart, FAICP, general editor. *Growing Smart Legislative Guidebook: Model Statutes for Planning and Management of Change.* Chicago: APA Planners Press, 2002.

2.   Ibid., Vol. 2, pp. 10-59.

3.   Arendt, Randall G. *Rural by Design: Maintaining Small Town Character.* Chicago: APA Planners Press, 1994.

PART

III

Day-to-Day
Operations

5

Getting Started: How to Set Up and Operate a Board of Adjustment

It is easy to overlook the procedures and operational matters and focus on the responsibilities of considering variances, conditional uses, and appeals. Some state-enabling legislation establishes membership requirements, while others leave such matters to each local government. It is important to consider the board's composition, the length of term for members, the procedure for how to handle vacancies, and other membership matters. The board should also have a set of bylaws, operating procedures for the numerous issues that ensure smooth sailing for the board, and good record keeping. This chapter will guide the board through these topics.

MEMBERSHIP

Many, but not all, states have specific membership requirements. The appointment of members to a board is a matter for the elected body. If the requirements for membership are not spelled out in an ordinance, resolution, or set of procedures, the board should recommend to the elected body that membership requirements be established.

The membership issues to consider include the following:

- Number of members;
- Representative or at-large membership;
- Alternate members; and

- Eligibility requirements.

Boards typically have five or seven members. Unless specified in state law, the number is not particularly important. In small communities, a smaller board may be desirable, as the pool of eligible members is small. The board should be large enough to represent the community, but not so large as to be unwieldy.

Board appointments are typically made by one of three methods:

1. Representing districts;
2. Representing professions; or
3. At large.

Some communities prefer to have each elected representative from a commission or council district appoint a member from that district to serve on the board. Other communities prefer to have a board composed of members who represent professions associated with planning and development (e.g., planners, architects, engineers, surveyors, attorneys, realtors, and environmentalists). The third method does not establish eligibility requirements based on residing in a council district or based on being a member of a particular profession; however, all members must reside within the local government jurisdiction that the board serves.

Some jurisdictions have found it helpful to appoint one or two alternate members to serve in the absence of regular members. This ensures that the board has a quorum when members are away, and ensures that a person is ready and available to step in when needed. Alternates typically attend board meetings and receive training just as regular members do.

BYLAWS

Most states require that a board adopt bylaws, which is a good idea. "Bylaws" are the rules adopted by the board to govern its members and regulate its affairs. The set of bylaws will typically address matters required by state law.

Bylaws should spell out the procedure for amending the bylaws, whether due to changes in statutory requirements or other changing circumstances. Bylaws should be adopted upon motion and vote of the board.

The following topics should be included in bylaws:

- Name of the board
- Authority for the board (a citation to any state-enabling legislation and local ordinances establishing the board)

- Definition of terms that have a particular meaning in the bylaws
- Membership matters, including qualifications, term of office, vacancies, removal from office, reimbursement of members for expenses, disqualification from voting, and oath of office
- Roles and responsibilities of the board
- Procedures for meetings and hearings, including quorum, frequency of meetings, regular meetings, called meetings, and the conduct of the meeting itself (or a requirement to adopt a set of procedures regarding the conduct of meetings and hearings)
- Procedures to amend the bylaws

OPERATING PROCEDURES

It is desirable to adopt a set of procedures that are separate from the bylaws. These more detailed rules may be adopted by motion of the board and should establish procedures describing how various board matters are handled (e.g., reimbursement of expenses, conduct of meetings, and record keeping). In fact, written procedures are a good idea for any operation of the board. Procedures do not have to be lengthy, complex, or legalistic. Rather, the reason for written procedures is to ensure that board members, the public, staff, and elected and appointed officials of the local government know how various operating matters will be handled.

For the topics identified here, the local government may have sets of procedures that apply to all employees, elected officials, and appointed officials. When this is the case, board members should have copies of these procedures to follow in carrying out their responsibilities. However, when the board is taking action on matters with no procedures, the board should adopt its own set of procedures.

Procedures should spell out the steps in a process to complete an action. For example, procedures for reimbursement might include identification of forms to be used, time for submitting requests, approvals needed, supporting documentation that is required, and identification of who handles the request. Procedures on all matters should be simply stated to ensure clear understanding and to supplement the legal requirements stated in the bylaws.

It is especially important to have a set of procedures for the conduct of meetings and hearings. (See Chapter 6 for a more detailed discussion of meetings and meeting management.)

RECORD KEEPING

Boards of adjustment have the responsibility to maintain accurate and complete records for the following three primary reasons:

1. *The local government should maintain an accurate or sufficient record of actions taken by the board.* A board often needs information on past actions regarding site planning, platting, or other development approvals for a parcel. Property owners or prospective buyers often need to search for information on decisions regarding variances and conditional uses that may affect the property. Enforcement officials may need to identify past approvals in researching potential zoning violations.

2. *Decisions of the board must be supported by the written record and public hearing testimony.* The written record includes the original application, staff reports, public and individual property owner notices, agency comments and recommendations, and written comments received from the public. If the board's decision is challenged in court, and a specific piece of information supporting its findings and conclusions is not in the record, the result may be adverse to the board's decision.

3. *Board decisions often include conditions for granting an approval.* Of course, conditional uses, by their very nature, are approved with a set of conditions. However, variances, special uses, and other matters that may come before a board may also be approved subject to conditions. If the board has not made a complete record of the case, including an accurate record of the conditions that accompany the approval, it may be difficult to properly enforce those conditions.

In some states, such as Kentucky, the state-enabling legislation requires that the board annually review and report on the status of conditional use permits. If records have not been made or maintained, it will be difficult to conduct this required review and produce the necessary reports. Whether required by state law or not, periodic review of approvals with conditions is a good idea to verify that conditions continue to be met.

Checklists Help in Record Keeping

There are several checklists that a board and its staff can use to ensure that proper records are created and maintained.

The first checklist addresses basic requirements for processing applications at the staff level. This checklist is general; it should be supplemented with specific statutory requirements for public notice

Table 5-1. Application Forms and Reports

✓	Item	Date
	If the zoning procedures include a preapplication meeting, a record of the meeting (the item that should be in the file is a form indicating who was present and the topics covered)	Date of the preapplication meeting
	The original application, all supporting information, exhibits, and the property owner's signature (if local regulations require a complete application before processing commences, additional information may be required, such as a deficiency letter and information to make the application complete)	Date received, date of deficiency letter, date determined complete
	Where an agent represents the property owner, a signed document designating the agent	Date received
	Staff analysis and report on the application, including supporting information	Date prepared, and the dates of any supplements or revisions

and hearing procedures that apply in your state. The application (or case) file should contain at least the items related to the application and preparation of a report about the application. It is helpful in tracking records to include the date that each action is taken. A log sheet (as illustrated in Table 5-1) could be placed in each file.

A checklist for the hearing will ensure that all actions are taken and records maintained for those actions (Table 5-2). A log sheet will help track actions as well as ensure that all appropriate steps have been taken. It may be helpful to supplement these checklists with a separate checklist that lists information unique to each action (Tables 5-3 and 5-4).

The board secretary or staff may want to consider preparing copies of these checklists and including a copy in each case file, checking off documents as they are placed in the files. It is also advisable to place a note card in the file to indicate if a document has been removed. It is just as important to keep track of the contents of the file as it is to ensure that appropriate documents are initially placed in the file.

Table 5-2. Public Hearing(s)

✓	Item	Date
	Proof of mailed notice to surrounding and adjacent property owners	Date that proof was received
	Posted notice (some jurisdictions require a photograph of posted signs on property that is the subject of an application)	Date that notice was posted
	Legal notice in the newspaper	Date(s) of publication
	Agenda for the public hearing	Date that agenda was prepared and distributed
	Copies of sign-in sheets or speaker's forms for those speaking at the public hearing	Date(s) of hearing(s)*
	Copy of the minutes of the hearing, or the portion of the minutes reflecting action on the application	Date(s) of hearing(s)*
	Verbatim transcript (if one was prepared)	Date(s) of hearing(s)*
	List of findings of the board as a basis for decision	Date(s) of hearing(s)*
	Any evidence (exhibits) presented at the hearing	Date(s) of hearing(s)*

*In the case of hearings that are continued, the date for each action should be included.

Log Books

Some local governments maintain log books to track cases. Such a log, or record, includes the case name, docket (or case) number, submittal date, hearing date, and final action. This log of board activities can be very useful to document a case file or for easy reference to answer information requests. In addition, it is a great way to note conditional use permits or variances that may have time-sensitive conditions or requirements. In this way, a quick glance through the log indicates what actions the board or its staff may need to take in order to remain current on its responsibilities.

Table 5-3. Conditional Use

✓	Item	Date
	Copy of the conditions attached to the approval (where local regulations require a signature by the property owner acknowledging the conditions, the file copy should be fully signed)	Date(s) of the hearing(s) where the action was taken
	Permit, if applicable, along with a transmittal letter to the property owner	Date of issuance
	Letters or notices sent to the property owner and other departments or agencies regarding final action	Date(s) of letters or notices
	Follow-up reports or inspections to verify compliance with conditions	Date of action

Table 5-4. Variance

✓	Item	Date
	Copy of any conditions attached to the approval	Date(s) of the hearing(s) where the action was taken
	Letter to the property owner regarding final action (approval or denial)	Date of issuance
	Letters or notices sent to other departments or agencies regarding final action	Date(s) of letters or notices
	Follow-up reports or inspections to verify compliance with conditions	Date of action

FOR MORE INFORMATION

Your local government may have forms and filing procedures well established. However, if the board needs assistance in addressing record-keeping requirements, one good source of information is a technical guidance paper provided to assist planners in New York State. While the recommendations are directly related to New York requirements, the tips on record keeping are good and the methods are transferable. The paper, *Record Keeping Tips for Zoning Administration* by James A. Coon (part of the Local Government Technical Series) is available from the Tug Hill Commission in Watertown, NY (http://www.dos.state.ny.us/lgss/pdfs/record.pdf).

The sources identified in Chapters 1 and 2 will also have information on record keeping to assist the board in setting up or revising its procedures.

6

Making the
Most of
Your Meetings

The primary interaction between the board of adjustment and the public occurs during hearings, and to a lesser extent during meetings and workshops. The board's business is conducted primarily during hearings for hearing, considering, and rendering decisions on applications. In addition to public hearings, the board may hold several types of meetings.

Public Hearings

Applications for matters authorized to the board are presented and considered and decisions are rendered at public hearings. There should be rules of procedure for all meetings and hearings. Where decisions are to be made, particular attention should be given to procedures that ensure due process. (See Chapter 8 for a discussion of due process and Chapter 9 for a discussion on public hearings.) Board members should know and follow legal principles regarding public hearings.

Public Meetings

Action is taken in public meetings on board matters, such as electing officers, adopting or amending procedures, receiving reports from staff or other board members, handling formalities such as setting the agenda, approving minutes, and scheduling workshops.

Workshops

Workshops are not public hearings and do not require that public comment be taken. The rules that the board sets will determine whether public comment is taken at workshops or only at public hearings.

There are many reasons for workshops:

* *Exploring issues.* Workshops provide an opportunity for sharing information, generating ideas to address growth and development in the community, as well as discussing lessons learned during the consideration of applications. This may be a time for brainstorming and generating new ideas. These workshops may be board workshops, public workshops, and joint workshops with other groups.

* *Looking back and looking forward.* This type of workshop may be held as a board retreat or regular workshop for the purpose of evaluating past actions as well as setting goals for the future. This is a good workshop to hold jointly with other groups to include discussions about expectations and results from the perspectives of the elected body and the planning commission.

This chapter focuses on general principles of meeting management. Most people involved in planning and development have experienced meetings that seem out of control, last too long, or have no apparent rules or procedures. To get the most from board meetings, they must be orderly and productive. This chapter is designed to guide board members through a well-run meeting.

EFFECTIVE MEETINGS

Effective meetings have several common elements, including:
* An appropriate location (the meeting place)
* Adequate equipment
* An agenda
* A set of procedures
* Appropriate leadership
* Adequate participation by the board
* Opportunity for participation by citizens

THE MEETING PLACE

Meetings and hearings may be held in chambers (i.e., the local government assembly room provided for public meetings and hearings by the elected body). A board may also have another space or have occasion to meet in other locations. The place for board meetings should be regularly used for all meetings, unless special circumstances indicate that another location should be used.

What special circumstances may dictate choosing another location?

• *Board retreats or workshops are often better when held in a different location than the regular meeting room.* Retreats and workshops may be more informal than public hearings; brainstorming, group interaction, and creativity will be enhanced in a more informal setting.

• *Controversial applications often generate large numbers of participants and may overflow the space in the regular meeting place.* When the board expects a crowd, a different meeting place should be chosen. The move to a new location should be announced well in advance to make sure that all participants know of the change in routine.

• *Complex projects may require the use of audiovisual equipment that is not available or easily provided in the regular meeting place.* When the board anticipates this situation, a location should be chosen that has the necessary equipment. This move to a new location should be widely publicized to make sure that all participants know about the change.

• *In a large jurisdiction, it may be desirable to meet in different regions from time to time.* This takes board hearings into the community and nearer to the citizens. Holding meetings in neighborhood locations creates good will in the community and increases participation.

While attention to the meeting place is important, special attention to the conditions of the meeting place should be made. There are several important factors to consider.

Where Will Board Members Sit?

When the board members sit on a dais or platform, they are separated from the audience. This is a more formal, and sometimes intimidating, arrangement. A typical arrangement exists when the board meets in the chambers used by the elected body. The dais makes it possible for members of the audience to see the board members more easily. The board deals with important matters and a formal seating arrangement reflects the gravity of the situation.

In small towns and rural communities, meeting places may not be so formal. The space may more closely resemble a large classroom, with the board seated on the same level as the audience, which is also acceptable. However, it is especially important in this situation to establish a regular room arrangement with a head table that serves as the board seating area. This establishes some formality to the setting, and is consistent with the importance of the matters that come before the board. In small towns where most residents know each other, some degree of formality is important to help avoid inappropriate interaction that may violate due process. (See Chapters 8 and 9 for important principles of due process and the conduct of public hearings.)

Where Is the Podium Placed for Use by Staff, Applicants, and Citizens?

This is often problematic in that podium placement interferes with the view from the audience to the board. As public hearings become more like proceedings in a courtroom, it is difficult to have a meeting run smoothly with a single podium. A person giving testimony needs to stand at the podium; however, when cross-examination occurs, the attorney or person posing questions should also have a podium.

One solution is to have two or three separate tables set in the front of the room. One table is provided for staff, unless staff is seated with the board on the dais or at the designated board table. One table is provided for use by an applicant and any others who will provide testimony for the applicant. Another table may be provided for organized opponents who wish to provide testimony. When this type of arrangement is established, each table should have at least one microphone. Where separate tables with microphones are provided, the podium provides a location for citizens to speak, whether they are for or against the application.

Is There a Designated Space for the Press?

Members of the press may not routinely attend board meetings. In some communities, the press will attend only when there is a hot or controversial issue. In other communities, there will often be a reporter from the local paper in most, if not all, hearings and meetings. Controversial issues may attract attention from television reporters.

In any case, it is helpful to think about press attendance, whether sporadic or routine. A press table, or reserved seating area, is helpful if one or more reporters routinely attend the hearings. A designated space for television cameras ensures that the presence of television reporters and camera operators does not unreasonably interfere with the ability of audience members to see the board or any graphics used in presentations.

A Final Thought

The space should be comfortable, well lit, have sufficient seating, and be arranged in such a manner as to eliminate potential barriers to participation by all parties. One way to address the arrangement of the space is to visit the room when other meetings are being conducted and experience the meeting from a different perspective. When problems or potential problems are identified, seek assistance from staff or elected officials to resolve them.

ADEQUATE EQUIPMENT

At a minimum, the room should have microphones and speakers in order to ensure that all participants can hear; devices to assist those with impaired hearing are also necessary. Provision for audio recorders, projectors, television monitors, video recorders, and computer projectors should be considered. Whatever is provided must be appropriately placed (see above discussion). Furthermore, it is important to consider electrical outlets and extension cords to provide power. It may be difficult to ensure an appropriate location to meet viewer needs while still ensuring adequate power. Extension cords can pose a safety hazard.

Recording Equipment

A staff person may be assigned as the board secretary who is responsible for taking minutes and ensuring an audio or video recording of the meeting or hearing. The room arrangement should make it possible for the board secretary to see board members in order to accurately record who is speaking and to better hear what is being said. Typically, the board secretary is taking minutes rather than writing a verbatim record. To accompany the minutes, an audio or video record may be prepared. Recording equipment should be located so that the board secretary can easily monitor the equipment, change tapes, or troubleshoot problems with the equipment. Typically, the board secretary is also responsible for the sound system, which may require troubleshooting as well.

In some instances, an applicant, opponent, or other interested party will hire a court reporter to record the testimony and discussion verbatim. Establishing an appropriate location for a court reporter as a routine part of the room arrangement will ensure that space is available, that there is minimal disruption when a court reporter needs to set up equipment, and that the presence of the court reporter does not interfere with the hearing.

Graphic Aids and Equipment

There are many things to think about in arranging a meeting space to accommodate a variety of graphic aids and presentation equipment:

• *Make sure that easels can be placed close enough to the board members for them to clearly see the information depicted on graphic boards.* It is often difficult or impossible to place easels where both the board and audience can view the graphics placed on the easel. Remember: the purpose of the graphics is to support or illustrate the verbal presentation. The graphic materials are evidence and must be seen by board members. (See Chapter 9 for a discussion of evidence.)

• *If overhead projectors are used, place the projector in such a way as to avoid blocking audience views of the board and the screen.* This is especially problematic because a person must place transparencies on the glass, which means that the person may also block views. It is particularly difficult for a presenter to handle the projector and transparencies and make the presentation. Careful attention to room arrangement and placement of an overhead projector will minimize interference with views by the projector and its operator.

• *Consider the placement of computer-aided presentations.* The computer and associated projector can often be operated by remote control. The equipment itself is smaller than most overhead projectors; however, placement is still an important issue. The presenter often needs to be able to see the computer screen rather than the projection screen. As with other graphics and graphic devices, careful attention in advance will ensure minimal disruption due to the equipment.

• *Pay attention to room lighting when selecting the location of screens and easels for graphics.* For presentation of flip charts or for high-tech computer projections, pay attention to the location and brilliance of light fixtures as well as windows. When there is a choice of meeting spaces, choose a space where the lighting can be controlled. Bright light on a projection screen makes it impossible to see the images. Dim light at the dais or in the audience makes it difficult to take notes. It may not be possible to strike a balance to meet all needs, but advance attention to this detail will help minimize the problem.

MEETING PREPARATION

Agenda

Every meeting should have an agenda. The agenda contains a list of matters to be considered and acted on by the board and the order in which such matters will be considered. It may also include statements about opportunities to speak, rules and guidelines for the conduct of the meeting, the availability of equipment or devices to meet special needs (hearing devices, for example), and how to appeal decisions. It is a good idea to have a standard agenda format, which is followed every time and helps ensure that no items are inadvertently omitted.

An agenda is part of the preparation for the meeting. Well-run meetings occur because of good preparation. Whether the agenda is prepared by staff or by the board chair, it should be available in advance of the meeting to both the public and to board members. In addition to a list of items to be considered and actions to be taken, the agenda should also identify the date of the meeting or hearing, the place, and the time. There must be enough copies available for the audience. Consider the need for providing the agenda in languages other than English. Finally, avoid jargon, acronyms, or other special terms that are not easily understood by the public.

A Set of Procedures

A set of procedures should be in place for the conduct of the meeting. The discussion on public hearings in Chapter 9 is concerned largely with what happens during a meeting that is an advertised public hearing. It is a good idea to have procedures on the conduct of every meeting. The procedures should address the ceremonial items that typically occur at the beginning of the meeting, how citizens are recognized to speak, and the order of appearance for matters related to applications.

There are two fairly common means of recognizing citizens who wish to speak on a matter before the board:

1. *Provide a form, either a card or a sheet of paper, for a citizen to sign up to speak.* The form should provide space for the name, address, phone number, affiliation of the speaker, and a space for the matter to be addressed. These forms are given to the board chair or the board secretary, according to the established procedure. When the time arrives for public comment, the chair or the secretary calls each name in the order received.

2. *Allow people to approach the podium when the public hearing portion of the meeting is announced.* It is a good idea to have a sign-in sheet on the podium to record the speaker's name and other information.

Procedures also address the order of presentations for matters requiring decisions by the board. The board attorney should assist in developing this procedure. One typical approach is the following:

• Presentation of the application by staff, with a brief summary of the report on compliance, and a staff recommendation (if recommendations are requested or required)

• Comment or additional presentation by the applicant, the applicant's agent or attorney, and witnesses

• Public hearing (opportunity for comment by the public)

• Questions from the board and discussion by the board

• Board findings and decisions

The procedures should also address the time limits established for each speaker and any other matters about the conduct of the meeting. (See Chapter 9 for specific information on quasi-judicial hearings.)

Appropriate Leadership

A meeting should have a beginning, a middle, and an end. Although this seems obvious, who has not attended a meeting that seemingly would never end? An important responsibility of the board chair is to lead the meeting, set the tone at the beginning, and maintain order and timeliness until the end. This means that all items on the agenda are addressed and that items are moved to conclusion.

The board chair is responsible for the tone of the meeting. The tone set by the chair will affect the orderliness of the proceeding. This means that the board chair should convey a sense of order and appropriate attitude, being impartial in matters before the board. (See the discussion on due process in Chapter 8.) By displaying this attitude, the chair can more effectively insist that other participants also behave appropriately and maintain order. The chair should not be weak or unfocused in the conduct of the meeting; on the other hand, the chair should not be too strong or intimidating. Even when a meeting has dragged on into the early morning hours, the chair should maintain an upbeat attitude. Continue to strive to be upbeat and positive, fair and courteous.

While the board attorney may be present, the chair also has a responsibility to ensure that all legal requirements are followed. One way to ensure that requirements are met is to adopt and follow a set of procedures.

The chair should make sure that everyone has a chance to be heard but still maintain a timely meeting through enforcement of time limits. During presentations, the chair should maintain the tone by quickly quelling outbursts, personal attacks, or other rude behavior.

Finally, the chair should be thoroughly familiar with the items on the agenda, which demonstrates the importance of the matters that come before the board. If the chair leads the board by preparing in advance, reading the agenda and all of the back-up material, and reading and studying the plan and regulations, the other board members will more likely follow through with their own preparation. Citizens will feel that matters of concern to them and their community are given appropriate attention.

Adequate Participation by the Board

Board members have a responsibility for the smooth running of an effective meeting. The chair obviously sets the tone and leads the meeting; however, each member is responsible in two ways:

1. Preparation for the meeting
2. Behavior during the meeting

A board member should be prepared. Read the material included with the agenda. Visit the site that is the subject of an application. (Note: Be sure to consult with the board attorney to determine whether such site visits are allowable in your jurisdiction. See the discussion on ex parte communications in Chapter 8, and the discussion on ethics related to ex parte communications in Chapter 7.)

Consult other materials for a clear understanding of the issues. An important aspect of preparation relates not to individual cases, but to being educated and informed about the kinds of matters that come before the board. Learn about variances and conditional uses and procedures from training and guidebooks, the Internet and print resources. The community's comprehensive or general plan, zoning and other regulations, and explanatory documents about such things as conditional uses or variances are important in order to understand the issues. (There are many resources to help understand how board matters are handled in each state. See the chapters in this book with sections entitled "For More Information" for guidance.)

You may wish to ask staff for clarification in order to understand the situation. To create an appropriate record, make such requests in writing. The staff response should also be in writing. Both the request and the response should be part of the record.

Board members have a responsibility for well-run meetings during the meeting or hearing itself. Be on time. Listen to the explanations by staff and ask questions if something is not clear. Listen to the applicant and citizens as evidence is presented. Ask questions for clarification but do not argue or voice opinions.

Several guidelines can help you during the meeting:

• Be polite and patient with others who are not familiar with public hearing procedures.

• Be patient with those who have a different opinion. Citizens have left the comfort of home to participate and deserve patience and respect for their opinion.

• Leave personalities behind.

• Be open minded and fair.

• Strike an appropriate balance between formality and informality. Do not use first names when addressing speakers, unless the person is well known to the board. (In a small community, this may be everyone!)

• Treat all speakers and participants in a similar fashion.

• Be patient with citizens who are not familiar with rules, planning jargon, and legal documents that board members understand from practice and training.

• Do not dominate the discussion. Make the points that need to be made and allow the discussion to continue.

• Be careful about the tone of voice. Meetings and hearings are not the place for sarcasm and anger. Board members should model the behavior that is expected from the public.

Above all, remember that this is not a debate. The board is there to hear testimony and make decisions based on evidence, not engage in a debate. The thoughtful and reasoned participation of each member is an important contribution to a well-run and effective meeting.

FOR MORE INFORMATION

• Cogan, Elaine. *Successful Public Meetings: A Practical Guide.* Chicago: APA Planners Press, 2000.

7

Ethics: Behavior and Decision-Making

Carol D. Barrett, FAICP

ETHICS ARE IMPORTANT

This chapter discusses the ethics of decision-making for board members. Ethics are the values and principles that govern our behavior. Board members work in an area where the stakes are high. For applicants, big money or major personal interests are at risk. For neighbors, emotions may be aroused. Citizens are protecting the sanctity of their neighborhoods, fearing traffic and other environmental impacts. An awareness of the ethical pitfalls and a personal commitment to act in an ethical manner are needed to preserve the public trust.

Variances give people permission to do something that is contrary to the requirements of the zoning regulations. It is a very powerful land-use tool that can, like all forms of power, be abused. Ethical principles, when commonly accepted by the board and coherently expressed to the community, can help the board act in a more ethical and responsible manner.

WHY IS IT HARD TO ALWAYS MAKE ETHICAL DECISIONS?

There are many reasons why ethical behavior is sometimes hard to achieve:

- The decisions of a board are collective. Group think and group speak tend to deter individual ethical awareness.

- A board is part of a larger governmental operational structure. A bureaucratic structure shields people from personal responsibility and accountability.

- There is often uncertainty as to what types of behavior are expected. There is little orientation and training for many new board members, and ethical training is even less common.

- Even a board member aware of ethical conundrums and wishing to act ethically may feel stymied by the observation that unethical conduct by others is tolerated.

Government can encourage ethical decisions by honestly and openly acknowledging this dimension of board work.

WHAT ARE THE STANDARDS FOR ETHICAL CONDUCT AND ADOPTION OF ETHICAL GUIDELINES?

For board members, there will be at least two sources of formal standards for ethical conduct:

1. Most states and many local governments have some type of ethics ordinances or laws.

2. "Ethical Principles in Planning," adopted by the American Planning Association, cover the activities of decision-makers in the planning process. The Principles emphasize serving the public interest and achieving high standards of integrity and proficiency.

"Ethical Principles in Planning" from the American Planning Association and Other Sources

The ethical principles are aspirational rather than a list of prohibitions or statements of explicit conduct. (The full text of the "Ethical Principles in Planning" may be found at the APA website (http://www.planning.org/ethics/ethics.html). The key points are:

A. Serve the public interest
1. Recognize the rights of citizens to participate in planning decisions.
2. Give citizens full, clear, and accurate information.
3. Expand choice and opportunity for all persons.
4. Assist in the clarification of community goals.
5. Ensure that information available to decision-makers is also available to the public.
6. Pay special attention to the interrelatedness of decisions and the long-range consequences of present actions.
B. Strive to achieve high standards of integrity and proficiency.
1. Exercise fair, independent, and honest judgment.

2. Publicly disclose any personal interests.
3. Define personal interest broadly.
4. Abstain from participation in a matter in which you have a personal interest and leave the chamber when that matter is being deliberated.
5. Seek no gifts or favors.
6. Abstain from participating as an advisor or decision-maker on any plan or project in which you have previously participated as an advocate.
7. Serve as an advocate only when the objectives are legal and serve the public interest.
8. Do not participate as an advocate on any plan or program in which you have previously served as an advisor or decision-maker except after full disclosure and in no circumstance earlier than one year following termination of the role as advisory or decision-maker.
9. Do not use confidential information to further a personal interest.
10. Do not disclose confidential information.
11. Do not misrepresent facts or distort information.
12. Do not participate in any matter unless prepared.
13. Respect the rights of all persons.

Board members should understand these expectations. Training as a member should include a review of ethical standards and examples of how to apply them in your work. The board can also take local action to affirm its acceptance of the aspirational standards embodied in the statement by adopting the statement.

It should be noted that these Principles are not enforceable and there is no legal sanction for failure to adhere to the standards. However, making a public commitment to doing the best job possible sets a tone for your deliberations. It also serves as advance notice as well as a useful refuge for the board from unwanted debate with those who might seek to encourage unethical behavior.

If the language or length of the American Planning Association statement doesn't fit within the operating style of your board, consider adopting a set of statements that resonate within your community. Adopting a statement is not an accusation that a board member has behaved unethically. The point is not assignment of blame; it is to emphasize the shared responsibility for achieving ethical conduct.

In smaller communities, it is inevitable that board members will have to make decisions that disappoint friends and business acquaintances. This also causes wear and tear on volunteers. Sometimes board members resign because they don't feel appreciated or they grow weary of the public criticism of tough decisions. Adopted ethical standards can be a way of addressing these problems by providing some protection against accusations based on the vague feeling about whether a decision was ethical.

The City of Minneapolis drafted a Code of Ethics (www.ci.minneapolis.mn.us/mayor/priorities/ethics/ethicsdraft.pdf, adopted in 2003) which include hortatory language worthy of consideration. The Code says:

Ethical Aspiration 1: Trust
1.   We put the public interest ahead of our own personal enhancement and financial interests.
2.   We disclose conflicts of interest and refrain from participating in decisions where we have a financial interest.
3.   We avoid actions that might impair independence of judgment or give the appearance of impropriety or a conflict of interest.
4.   We do not use our positions to gain privileges or special treatment and do not use public property or personnel for private or personal purposes.

Ethical Aspiration 2: Fairness
1.   We act honestly, fairly, and openly so that others can rely in good faith on our words and actions.
2.   We do not engage in or tolerate discrimination, retaliation, harassment, or abuse.
3.   We maintain and respect confidentiality and decide all matters based on their merits, free from improper influence.

Ethical Aspiration 3: Accountability
1.   We comply with both the letter and the spirit of applicable Federal and State law and regulations, the City Charter, the Minneapolis Code of Ordinances, and City policies and procedures.

Ethics Ordinances

Government ordinances tend to regulate two categories of activities:

1. Those that require disclosure of information, such as sources of income; and

2. Those that prohibit certain conduct.

Prohibited Conduct

• *Solicitation or Acceptance of Gifts.* Board members should not solicit or accept items of value when it is based on an understanding that their judgment would be influenced by the gift. The prohibition against acceptance should apply in those circumstances when a reasonable person might make the inference that the vote was influenced. (Specific dollar limitations on gifts may vary by jurisdiction or by state.)

> *Example:*
> **Q.** *Can you accept the use of a vacation condominium from a developer who has no cases currently pending before the board although he has sought relief in the past?*
> **A.** No. Acceptance of such a gift, even if unsolicited, would leave the impression that you were indebted to the developer and you might unconsciously be influenced in the future.

• *Misuse of Position.* Board members cannot use their positions to solicit special privilege for themselves or for others. They are not to disclose, for their specific benefit, confidential information gained through their position.

• *Conflict of Interest.* Patty Salkin, Director of the Government Law Center of Albany Law School, suggests that communities provide board members, prior to their appointment and then once a year for an update, with forms that would help people identify a predilection for conflicts. The following questions should be addressed:

1. Does your business operate in a way that it could come before the board, or could it benefit or be harmed by a decision made by the board?

2. Are you or a member of your family engaged in a profession that could bring you or them before the board?

3. Are you a member of one of these professions: planner, engineer, architect, surveyor, realtor, or attorney?

4. Does your business benefit indirectly from decisions made by the board (e.g., mortgage broker, contractor, or building materials sale)?

A "yes" to any of the four questions above does not create an automatic problem, but is something to be aware of and might, in some cases, indicate a reason for not accepting an appointment.

A person should pay attention to these matters because there will often be a perception of a conflict when there are overlapping interests (although not necessarily financial). Answering the questions honestly will show you where the public may believe there is a conflict of interest.

Examples of public accusations of conflict of interest can occur when you live near a project coming before the board, or when you have a position in the community that establishes your values and support for an entity that is making a request of the board.

Trouble can arise when there are gut feelings about the rightness or wrongness of a circumstance that can't be covered in law:

• Is it wrong that the board grants a variance to the sister of the board's chair?

• Is it wrong that a board member who is known to have a public beef with an applicant gets to vote on the conditional use permit?

When reflecting on whether there is a conflict, there are broader questions about whether you are biased that are rarely covered in law. To help you respond to various circumstances, ask yourself the following questions:

• Do the circumstances of the case make you uncomfortable?

• Would the public perceive the circumstances as influencing your decision?

> *Examples:*
>
> **Q.** *Can a nursing home volunteer vote on an application by a hospice, which receives patients from the nursing home?*
>
> **A.** There is no remuneration involved. The member works as a volunteer. Practically speaking, you would not want to set limits on volunteer activities. Anyone too insulated from community life wouldn't make a good board member. Volunteers are likely to have information and opinions about matters that come before them, but that does not preclude thoughtful analysis or decisions.
>
> **Q.** *If you vote on a variance for a project that offers shopping near a neighborhood where your widowed elderly mother lives, is that a conflict of interest because she would now have stores more conveniently located?*
>
> **A.** No. The benefit is extremely indirect. By that standard, one would benefit from any new store in town that improved the number of places where you can shop.

In smaller jurisdictions, with only one to two major employers, the applicant may also employ relatives who are in some way connected to the board members. Is it a conflict of interest? Maybe. It would depend on the circumstances. In larger communities, you have a large enough pool of volunteers to eliminate most obvious or apparent conflicts of interest; in small cities or towns, that is not possible. Having board members alert to the possibility of conflicts, and addressing them in a thoughtful and forthright fashion, will go a long way toward providing a foundation for ethical conduct.

Examples:

Q. *In the case of the Fordsam University, would it be a conflict of interest for a retired university librarian who sits on the board to vote on a variance to permit the construction of a new physics lab without the required setbacks and parking?*

A. As stated, it would not be a conflict because the project would have no discernible impact on the librarian as distinct from any other member of the community. However, it could present a conflict of interest if the librarian were closely related to a professor in the department who would get a new lab in the proposed building. It would also present a conflict of interest if her son were currently employed in the professor's laboratory.

Q. *A board member owns a recreational vehicle (RV) park across the street from a proposed concrete plant seeking a variance from the city's noise standards. The member is distressed and, in a series of meetings with key city officials, aggressively questions the legality of the request. Other board members may be aware of the meetings. The night of the concrete plant variance hearing, the RV owner excuses himself from the discussion and leaves the room. Did his other actions create a conflict of interest circumstance for the board?*

A. No. The board member withdrew from making the decision but is not precluded from having questions and opinions as a private citizen. His contacts were with city staff, and all citizens are able to direct inquiries to city employees. The nature of his business is probably already known to the other board members.

Voting on matters when there is a financial conflict of interest is prohibited. The prohibition applies when the gain would accrue to one's employer, family, or an entity from which one derives a significant portion of one's income. For every state and many local governments, there is often a specific definition for a financial conflict of interest, which covers the amount of money and which relatives are defined as a member of the family.

If you have a conflict, state law generally requires disclosure. You may be prohibited from participating in any manner in making the decision and from communicating with anyone who is involved in making the decision. Some people feel they should leave the room until the matter is settled. Rarely do laws require vacating your place, but there are many ways that you can communicate a preference to your fellow board members, perhaps even inadvertently. In matters of conflict, you must seek advice from the board attorney on proper behavior.

State law is generally written around an economic conflict of interest where you or members of your family derive special economic benefits from the decision. What if the conflict is about philosophical, political, or religious beliefs? Even though these may affect your decision, they are not defined under state law as requiring disclosure and abstention from participation. On the other hand, although not regulated by state law, these do require your careful consideration. You must ask yourself whether you can be completely honest and impartial. If you cannot, you should declare that you have a personal conflict and withdraw.

Being attentive to these matters is not a reason to avoid taking a position on controversial matters in the community. Take a few minutes when reviewing your agenda packet to look for conflicts and think about their resolution ahead of the meeting. However, insincere, self-reported fears of a conflict of interest should not be used as a cop-out to avoid taking action on a controversial decision.

What about board members who have participated in political campaigns? Political support for good public policy (e.g., affordable housing and preservation of creeks) doesn't preclude fairly evaluating project requests. Soliciting money from those who appear before the board in support of these endeavors could be a problem.

Example:

Q. *You are asked to have your name appear on a list of political supporters for a candidate for council running on a platform limiting all new development.*

A. You should not take a public stand on limiting new development, which would have the impact of implying that you will not approve future variance requests as a means of stopping growth.

Ex Parte Communications

Ex parte communications occur outside of the formal meeting. (See Chapter 8 for a discussion of the legal issues in ex parte communications.) Prohibitions against such contact vary by state. You should request information on your local constraints as part of learning about your job.

Why is it a problem when information is communicated to you outside of a meeting?

- Not everyone has the same information.
- The applicant cannot respond if accusations are made.
- You cannot readily assess the accuracy of the information by seeking confirmation from staff.
- It violates the perceived fairness of process if special information has been conveyed to a subset of the board membership.

Some board members profess that they are comfortable with receiving communications from the project's neighbors or other concerned citizens. They believe that being open to community input is part of their job. Those members explain that they report the ex parte communications prior to the beginning of the official meeting. However, disclosure may not be enough. You cannot easily convey the full text of information received or the way you may have been influenced.

Site visits are a form of ex parte communication; however, they may be desirable. They can take the form of individuals driving by a site or exploring it alone on foot. Some communities choose to organize group visits with staff. Because you may have a quorum of planning commissioners present, such site visits should be posted as a public meeting. Staff should prepare a brief write-up of the visit for the public record. While on the site, board members should maintain an open mind and refrain from offering opinions to the property owner who is likely to be present.

Serial Meetings

Serial meetings may be prohibited by state or local ethics codes. Whether precluded or not, they should be avoided. Serial meetings are the product of high technology, particularly e-mail. As board members know, meetings where decisions are made have to be conducted in public. A serial meeting occurs when a series of e-mails among board members results in a debate and discussion of a pending case. E-mails about pending matters should be avoided.

Disclosure

Bias results when you use your position to make decisions that affect your personal financial interests. This is why some jurisdictions require public officials such as board members to disclose their financial interests. Completing the annual disclosure form reminds board members where potential conflicts exist. Communities that adopt disclosure requirements are saying that you are expected, when you accept appointment, to put your public interest above personal considerations.

Not every community requires disclosure; among those that do, different financial levels may trigger disclosure. In your training, be sure by requesting information; assistance from the Office of the Clerk or the board attorney may also be available. Please remember that jurisdictions which require disclosure also have penalties for failure to comply. Disclosure statements are also public documents and are the subject of open records act requests.

The types of information that may require disclosure include:
- Gifts
- Real estate owned, other than your home
- Stocks and bonds
- Businesses owned, even if the ownership is only in part
- Employer
- Other sources of income

HOW TO ENSURE AN ETHICAL BODY

Appointments

There are several things communities can do to help ensure an ethical board. First, you must concern yourself with the appointment process. The appointment of talented, community-serving, and competent individuals will go a long way to ensure ethical conduct.

A list of the personal qualities that you would want in a fellow board member would undoubtedly include the following:
- Fair, objective, and open minded
- Able to understand and consider long-range and interrelated decisions
- Unlikely to have conflicts of interests with matters coming before the board
- Able to act with integrity
- Hard working and comes to all meetings prepared to vote
- Places community interests before special interests

In some communities, there is a tradition of appointing members who represent the community's vision and values as determined by the most recent election. There is not anything inherently wrong with this approach, but it makes the job of a board member more challenging:

- There may be a higher-than-average turnover, which results in the need for training and down time for the group as new members learn the ropes.

- It further strengthens the notion that political factors influence the decision more than the facts of the case. This can make it more challenging to create an atmosphere of mutual trust and respect among the board members and between the community and the board.

Before agreeing to serve as a board member, you should consider what your community is trying to accomplish with the people who are appointed. Depending on the local government's organizational scheme, board members may represent a geographic area or be appointed at large. The appointing body may say, "Good luck and work hard," or they may instead expect you to check in regularly. Your job will be made easier or more difficult by the caliber and integrity of those who sit next to you at the table. You want to have members with commitment to your community and with values, but those values should not be expressed as biases in doing the board's work. (For further discussion on communication among citizen partners in planning, see Chapter 2.)

Example:

Q. *Is it appropriate for a board member who chairs the city's Greenbelt Alliance to fail to grant a waiver to the parkland dedication requirement, even when the standards of the variance are met by saying, "You meet the requirements for a variance, but I'm just not comfortable voting in favor of it."*

A. No. That would be an example of one's values expressing themselves as a bias.

Training

A community should provide ethics training or even mandate an ethics seminar upon appointment and regularly thereafter. Such training is available locally and nationally through the American Planning Association. Publications and books can be studied at your leisure and at less expense. Staff can provide you with the necessary resources.

By-laws and Rules of Procedure

Boards should have by-laws and rules of procedure. (Refer to Chapter 5 for further discussion on adopting procedures.) Copies of the rules should be available for the public at each meeting so first-timers understand what is going to happen. The advantage of having rules, and then operating according to the published standards, is that it creates consistent expectations. This goes a long way toward ensuring both the public and the applicant that they are receiving fair treatment.

Rules of procedure can also make a clear statement about how the board expects to be treated by others. For example, the rules can advise people that it is improper to contact board members outside of the public meeting about matters that are under consideration by the board.

There is another benefit to careful construction of rules of procedure and then following the rules: it is the best protection in the event that lawsuits are filed against the jurisdiction or against you personally.

Some communities also find it helpful to have written expectations for demeanor. The City of Denver in its discussion of the board of adjustment writes:

> It should be remembered that because of the inherently stressful nature of the proceedings, emotions often run high and patience is strained. Therefore, a calm attitude, courtesy, and respect will contribute greatly to a smooth and judicious hearing. Since (sic) this is a quasi-judicial body, conduct and apparel appropriate to a Court of Law is proper (no applause, no outbursts).[1]

Besides having rules, and following them, the actual public hearing and the decision-making process should be conducted in a way that maximizes everyone's confidence in the process and provides fair treatment for all parties. The goal is to have full and open consideration of the request, which entails demonstrating that the board is impartial, free from outside influence, and able to hear all voices— the quiet voices as well as the influential. (Refer to Chapter 9 for legal issues in decision-making.)

The job of the member, once the hearing is underway is to:
- Hear the facts and assess their accuracy.
- Balance obligations under the community's development regulations.
- Consider neighbors' concerns.

- Assess the request against the standards in the ordinance.
- Render a decision.

Members should keep in mind that the proceedings of the board may be subject to all public information requirements and open records act requests. Perhaps the most stringent expectations arise in Florida where the Sunshine laws define two or more members discussing the case as a public meeting (see Chapter 286, Florida Statutes).

WORKING WITH PLANNING STAFF AND THE COMMUNITY

Just as there are principles of ethical conduct for board members, there are guidelines for planners, and a Code of Ethical Conduct for planners who have been examined and accepted by the American Institute of Certified Planners. Board members should acquaint themselves with these materials to better understand the frame of reference that staff members bring to their work.

Briefly noted, most planners undertake their work with a view toward making a difference in the future of their communities. The circumstance calls for mutual respect. For example, questions are to be expected, but it is not necessary to do so in a manner that attacks the intelligence and good intentions of staff.

The same suggestions apply to the members' relations with the community. Take time to understand their philosophy and treat their views with courtesy, especially when you do not share their perspective and you will be making a recommendation contrary to their request. Planners have responsibility to serve the public interest, which means they will not be able to adjust the facts to meet political objectives. Rules cannot be changed according to the social status of applicants.

SERVING THE LONG-RANGE PUBLIC INTEREST

Every decision of the board should be directed to serving the community's long-range interest. This standard should have the greatest weight even when balanced against private property rights, sentiments of those testifying either for or against the request, and other important community values that may arise from time to time.

Another way you can test yourself as to whether your decision will serve the long-range public interest is to answer the query: Will this decision ultimately have reasonably foreseeable negative consequences to the public that can be avoided by some other alternative or by a denial?

> *Example:*
> Q. *Should you grant a variance to roadway dedication require-ments if it will have no discernible short-term impact on the community?*
> A. No. The design and provision of streets is a basic responsi-bility of local government, and planning for the transporta-tion network is always going to be long range. Securing donations of right of way as development occurs is vital to the community's long-range interests.

How Long is "Long Range"?

As a guideline, when considering the long-range interest in granting variances, the impacts must be foreseeable. A good rule of thumb would be to consider the likely impacts (if any) that would occur within a decade.

What is the Public Interest?

At its most basic level, the interest of the public includes housing affordable to all members of the community; opportunities for work-ing, shopping, and recreating; a healthy environment; a well-designed built environment; and increased choice and opportunity for those with little.

WHAT HAPPENS WHEN
YOU HAVE ETHICAL QUESTIONS?

Questions about compliance with local/state ordinances and ethics codes can often be answered by a local or state ethics commission. Each body will have its own procedures for making an inquiry. The advice can be helpful in terms of complying with a legal mandate. Copies of published opinions may be available for your perusal as you familiarize yourself with the job of a board member.

If a local government or state has adopted an ethics code, it proba-bly has a provision for complaints, which will entail investigation. You should be prepared for such inquiries as part of doing the job. Each jurisdiction will have formal procedures for investigation of complaints. For board members, an irksome trend is for neighbors aggrieved by a decision to report an ethics violation when it is more of a circumstance in which reasonable individuals could disagree. While such allegations are often painful (particularly when they are reported to the media), if you have done your job properly, you will emerge from the process with a real sense of accomplishment.

What if your question is about the aspirational content of your job (e.g., serving the public interest)? Ask yourself a quick question: How would my mom feel if this were published on the front page of the hometown paper? If you are not proud of the alternative you are preparing to support, then you have additional work to do. Perhaps conditions should be imposed, the applicant could present a more creative alternative, or the item should be tabled for additional information.

REAL LIFE EXAMPLES:
QUICK QUESTIONS AND ANSWERS

Q. *Can a board member purchase a home from an individual who frequently appears before the board?*

A. You may, but certain precautions should be taken. During the period of time from when you contact the realtor to when the purchase is completed, you must declare that you have a conflict of interest on any item when the realtor appears before the board. You must be careful not to use your position as a board member to advance your personal interests beyond those of any other client. To make sure, the purchase price and the real estate commission should be comparable to other properties. If you are in search of a real "deal," you need to find a realtor who does not appear before you so that there will be no allegations that you were provided a special opportunity in exchange for future favors.

Q. *I'm an attorney on a board. To what extent am I required to abstain from matters involving a client of a client?*

A. While an attorney should always act within the guidance provided by the American Bar Association, a good rule of thumb would be to determine if you have a financial interest in the decision, which is different from its effect on members of the public in general. For example, a vote to vary the landscaping requirements for a new, privately built baseball stadium, when the applicant is a client of an accounting firm that uses your firm for legal services, would not produce a financial benefit to you different from the public at large. In this circumstance, you would not have to abstain. On the other hand, a vote to grant a use variance for a major development when the applicant would then have extensive need of financial accounting services, which would have the potential for increasing business to you, could constitute a conflict of interest and would require recusal.

Q. *Can I vote on a variance for a homeowner renovation located in my neighborhood?*

A. If you are within the standard notification boundary (for example, 200 feet from the property), the state notification requirements have already determined that you have a specific—not a general—interest in the property. Therefore, declaring a personal conflict would be preferred. If you are outside of the notification boundary, you may participate. Individual discretion should be used if you are close to the notification boundary.

Q. *I own a small general contracting business and serve on the board. Can I approach applicants about doing work for them after their case has been decided?*

A. No. Waiting until after the case is decided would not address the appearance of a conflict of interest. Many people would assume that there had been a quid pro quo (i.e., that your vote had been exchanged for future work).

Note

1. http://www.denvergov.org/BOA, then select "Hearing Conduct."

IV

Legal Principles

8

Much To Due
About Process

BASIC PRINCIPLES

When the board considers applications for variances, conditional uses, or administrative appeals, it is functioning in a court-like manner. Consequently, board meetings at which such applications are considered are frequently called "quasi-judicial hearings." Because decisions reached in a quasi-judicial hearing affect how a property owner can utilize his property, the board must comply with certain "due process" requirements, which are intended to ensure that all parties involved in a hearing before the board are treated fairly.

Most local governments have adopted rules of procedure by which the board conducts its hearings on applications for variances, conditional uses, and administrative appeals. It is essential that each board member become familiar with all adopted rules of procedure. (The need for procedures is discussed in Chapter 5.)

In addition to becoming familiar with any local rules of procedure, there are certain due process concerns that the board must address when deciding whether to grant or deny an application for a variance, conditional use, or administrative appeal. These concerns include:

- Providing adequate and proper notice of the hearing;
- Ensuring that each board member is an unbiased decision-maker; and

- Disclosing all ex parte communications received by each board member. (See the discussion on ethics in Chapter 7.)

Failure to properly address each of the above concerns could result in a court invalidating the board's decision.

ADEQUATE AND PROPER NOTICE

A fundamental requirement of any hearing is that adequate notice of the hearing be provided to the applicant and to the general public. The manner in which notice is required to be provided varies from state to state and from local government to local government. Typical methods of notice include publishing it in a newspaper, posting a sign on the property, and mailing a letter to the applicant and property owners located within a certain proximity to the property for which the application has been filed.

Notice to individuals other than the applicant is necessary because any decision of the board has the potential of affecting the owners of adjacent and nearby properties. Notice to these individuals must be provided far enough in advance so that such individuals will have a reasonable amount of time to become familiar with the application and to prepare for the hearing.

Failure to comply with adopted notice requirements places any decision reached by the board at risk. Indeed, improper notice is one of the most frequent reasons why a court invalidates a board's decision.

Occasionally, even though notice was properly provided pursuant to the adopted requirements, the applicant or opponents of the application may request that the hearing be postponed for a brief period of time to allow for preparation. This may also occur when witnesses are unavailable to attend the scheduled hearing. The board should grant a request for a continuance under such circumstances unless there have been multiple requests, or the applicant or an opponent can demonstrate that the granting of a continuance will cause substantial harm to that individual. It is rare, however, when a brief continuance of two weeks or even one month will cause substantial harm to either the applicant or an opponent.

ENSURING THAT EACH BOARD MEMBER
IS AN UNBIASED DECISION-MAKER

Each board member acts like a judge whenever he considers whether to grant or deny an application for a variance, conditional use, or administrative appeal. Consequently, just like a judge, each board

Continuing a Public Hearing

The following is an example of how *not* to treat a request for a continuance. In a hotly contested hearing that had lasted until 1:00 AM, one of the parties requested that the hearing be continued on another date due to the lateness of the hour. Additionally, the court reporter had been working for nearly seven hours and had become ill.

Rather than calmly considering the request, the chair attacked the party making the request, stating that the party had orchestrated the illness of the court reporter. In order to fully demonstrate her disgust at the party's request, the chair made a motion that the hearing be postponed until Christmas morning at 8:00 AM.

This type of conduct is unwarranted and should be avoided. It is unreasonable to require parties or board members to continue a hearing during the wee hours of the morning. It is also unreasonable to attempt to reschedule a hearing on a holiday. Such conduct may result in a court overturning the board's decision.

Although not related directly to due process concerns, this example raises another consideration for the board. Court reporters are entitled to periodic breaks during a hearing and should not be expected to perform their duties at 1:00 AM or while ill. In light of the important role that a court reporter performs (e.g., creating a verbatim transcript of the hearing), the board should treat the court reporter with respect and courtesy.

member must be an unbiased decision-maker (i.e., there are no circumstances that would compel or persuade the board member to vote in a particular manner). If such circumstances exist, the board member is not allowed to vote on the pending application. Rather, the board member must recuse himself, which means that the board member will not be voting on a particular application.

Two of the most common reasons for a board member not being allowed to vote on a pending application:

1. They have a financial interest in the pending application; and
2. They are a relative of either the applicant or an opponent.

These reasons are frequently referred to as a "conflict of interest" and make a lot of sense if considered in the context of a judicial proceeding. None of us would want to argue our lawsuit in court in front of a judge who is employed by our opponent or, even worse, who is a family member of the opponent. The same concerns exist for those individuals who appear before the board.

Each board member should review the agenda and/or board packet as soon as they are available so the board member can determine whether he has a conflict of interest. If a conflict of interest exists, the board member should disclose it as soon as possible. In those states that utilize alternate board members, early disclosure may allow an alternate board member to fill in for the "conflicted" board member. Similarly, if other board members have indicated that they will be unable to make the board meeting, announcing a conflict early will allow the parties and the remaining board members to determine whether the meeting should be rescheduled in order to achieve a quorum.

Occasionally, a board member will not learn that he has a conflict of interest until the hearing has begun. For example, sometimes the applicant is a corporate entity, such as Developers, Inc., rather than a person. The agenda and the board packets simply stated that the applicant is Developers, Inc. Yet, once the hearing begins, a board member may learn that three of his cousins are the owners and officers of Developers, Inc. Once the board member discovers this information and realizes that he has a conflict of interest, the board member is required to announce that he has a conflict and state the grounds for such conflict. The board member must then recuse himself.

Many states have statutory requirements with which a board member must comply if that member decides he cannot vote on a pending application. These requirements must be strictly followed.

There is nothing inappropriate about having a conflict of interest. Indeed, it will happen from time to time, especially in a small community. Failure to disclose the conflict of interest can, however, jeopardize the board's decision if it is challenged in court, and can result in an ethical violation by the board member.

EX PARTE COMMUNICATIONS

Each board member is supposed to base his decision regarding a pending application on the evidence that is presented during the board's meeting. Sometimes, however, individuals involved with a pending application will attempt to discuss the pending application with a board member before the hearing begins. Such communications are frequently referred to as "ex parte communications."

In most jurisdictions, a board member is supposed to avoid having ex parte communications regarding a pending application. In order to ensure a level playing field for the applicant and any opponents to the application, all information regarding a pending application must be provided to the board member during the hearing.

This requirement is based upon the judicial role that each board member performs while making a decision on a pending application. The rationale is easily understood in the context of a trial that occurs in court. It is understood by everybody involved in the lawsuit that nobody is entitled to have private conversations with the judge about his case. The concern is that one party may provide incorrect or improper information to the judge without the other party's knowledge, and the judge may base his decision upon such information. By requiring all communications to be made in the presence of all parties, everybody has full knowledge of the information that has been presented to the judge and, if necessary, has an opportunity to refute such information.

The same concern exists for board members. If a board member has private discussions about a pending application, such discussions may contain inaccurate information upon which a board member could base his decision. Yet, because such inaccurate information was conveyed in private, the other parties would never know about it and, consequently, would never have an opportunity to refute the incorrect information.

For example, suppose an application is pending for a special exception for a neighborhood commercial use. The property on which the use would be located contains a nesting osprey. However, a few of the opponents to the proposed neighborhood commercial use mistakenly believe that the nesting osprey is a bald eagle, and inform each board member of that fact, each of whom is an avid bird watcher and would never vote to allow an eagle's nest to be disturbed. Without being informed about those private communications, the applicant would be denied the opportunity to correct the mistaken information.

Although each board member is supposed to avoid ex parte communications, they still occur, particularly in small communities. Almost every board member has experienced standing in line at the supermarket while another shopper begins chatting about a pending application, especially on controversial proposals. When this occurs, the board member should attempt to terminate the discussion as quickly as possible by explaining that it is inappropriate for the board member to have such conversations.

There is an easy way to cure the problem of ex parte communications once they have occurred. If a board member receives a letter, it should be placed in the application file. If the board member is cornered at the supermarket, the board member should disclose and describe the ex parte communication at the beginning of the hearing on the pending application (e.g., the person involved in the communication, the date of the communication, and the substance of the communication). Additionally, the board member should indicate whether he is capable of basing his decision solely on the evidence presented during the hearing. If not, the board member should recuse himself from hearing that particular application. All parties should be provided an opportunity to ask the board member questions about the communication if they so desire.

Another approach to handling ex parte communications is for the board member to prepare a brief memorandum that describes the relevant information. This memorandum should be placed in the application file and made available to anybody who wants to review it. If there are numerous ex parte communications, this approach may be too burdensome to utilize. However, at a minimum, disclosure must be made at the outset of the hearing on the pending application.

Private site visits by a board member prior to the hearing may also fall within the category of ex parte communications, even if the board member was alone during the site visit. (This varies widely from state to state.) Although nobody discussed the pending application with the board member during the private site visit, the board member still obtained information prior to the hearing. This is contrary to the requirement that each board member must base his decision upon the evidence presented during the hearing. The rationale is the same as for private communications, where the board member may perceive something incorrectly during the site visit and base his decision on the incorrect information without providing the parties an opportunity to correct the erroneous perception.

The best way to address the problem with private site visits is to schedule and advertise the site visit so that all members of the board, as well as the applicant and any other interested parties, can visit the site at the same time. If this approach is used, discussion among the board members or the parties should not occur while they are at the site. Rather, all discussion should occur at the place where the board conducts its meetings.

Although potentially troublesome, ex parte communications can be easily resolved if each board member keeps in mind the problem associated with such communications. By disclosing the substance of the ex parte communications, everybody involved in the hearing will have an opportunity to address any incorrect information contained in the communication. This will ensure that the board member will not base his decision on erroneous information, and will result in a level playing field for all parties involved in the hearing.

FOR MORE INFORMATION

Chapter 1 contains a list of sources of information useful to board members. Several of these sources provide detailed information about the state requirements that ensure due process. Board members should also consult the board attorney for any questions regarding notice, conflict of interest, and ex parte communication.

9

A Time to Decide

Notice has been properly provided; the staff report has been final-
ized and distributed to the board members, the applicant, and all
interested parties; the hearing room has been carefully selected and
set up. It is now time for the hearing to commence. This chapter will
address what occurs during the board's hearing.

A party appearing before the board during a public hearing is generally entitled to:

- A sufficient opportunity to present evidence;
- Testimony provided while under oath;
- A right to cross-examination;
- An opportunity to rebut the opponent's arguments; and
- The entry of a written order with findings of fact and conclu-
sions of law.

Although some states do not mandate each of these requirements,
all of them will be addressed in this chapter. It is essential that the
board check with its attorney to determine which of these requirements are applicable in its jurisdiction.

PRESENTATION OF EVIDENCE

The board must base its decision on evidence that is presented during the hearing (as discussed in Chapter 8). That statement, however,
begs the question of what is evidence, and how a board member
should evaluate evidence.

What is Evidence?

Simply stated, "evidence" is any information that is presented to the
board during its hearing. The testimony of a witness is evidence, as

are pictures, staff reports, photographs, and other documents. The board must evaluate all of these forms of evidence when reaching its decision.

WITNESSES

Expert Witnesses

An expert witness is somebody who, based upon his experience or training, has special knowledge. It is typical for an engineer, a planner, or a landscape architect to testify as an expert witness in regard to proposed development. Expert witnesses can testify about their opinions, which must be based upon their area of expertise. Thus, a transportation engineer is entitled to provide an opinion about the carrying capacity of a roadway, but cannot provide an opinion about the environmental attributes of a proposed storm water system.

Layperson Witnesses

A layperson can also be a witness. A typical layperson witness is a homeowner who lives in the neighborhood in which a development is proposed to be located. A layperson cannot provide his opinion about a particular issue; opinions can only be provided by expert witnesses. Rather, a layperson must provide fact-based testimony about matters in which the layperson has first-hand knowledge.

The distinction between opinion-based testimony and fact-based testimony can be summarized as follows:

• An expert witness can state that, in his opinion, a proposed project will not adversely affect the viability of an endangered species. In order to provide such an opinion, the expert witness would have to rely upon his years of training and experience. Such an opinion could not be formulated without such training and experience.

• A layperson does not have the training and expertise to provide an opinion about the viability of an endangered species. Layperson testimony about such a topic is not credible because of this lack of professional training and expertise to render such an opinion. Accordingly, a layperson is limited to providing fact-based testimony about matters within his personal knowledge (e.g., statements about how many accidents have occurred at a particular intersection, the types of uses in the neighborhood, the heights and sizes of buildings near a proposed development, and the existence of endangered or threatened species). As long as the layperson has actual knowledge about a factual matter, he is entitled to provide such information to the board.

All evidence should be relevant to the matter pending before the board (i.e., the evidence should pertain to an issue related to the pending application). All too often, members of the general public will attempt to discuss matters that are not truly related to the pending application. When that occurs, it is the responsibility of the chair of the board to politely request that the witness stay focused upon the matter at hand.

How to Evaluate the Testimony of a Witness

The difficulty for a board member lies in determining how to evaluate the evidence that is presented during a hearing. This becomes particularly difficult in a hearing in which an application is contested by the neighbors. In such circumstances, it is common for the neighbors to attempt to counter the position of the applicant through the testimony of their own expert and layperson witnesses.

For example, the applicant's expert witness will often state that the proposed project is compatible with the neighborhood, while the neighbors' expert witness will state that the proposed project is not compatible. Evaluating such conflicting testimony is perhaps the most difficult task of a board member.

When confronted with conflicting testimony by expert witnesses, a board member should consider the following factors:

• Is the expert witness qualified to render the opinion provided to the board? Does the expert witness have the expertise and training to testify about the disputed issue?

• Is one expert witness better qualified than the other expert witness? This can be determined by evaluating the breadth of experience and training of each expert witness.

• Is the expert witness recognized as one of the stars in his profession? Does the expert witness frequently lecture at seminars and write articles regarding his area of expertise? Has the expert witness received special recognition or status from his professional association?

• How much time did the expert witness spend evaluating the proposed project? Did the expert witness only visit the site while driving to the hearing?

If each of the expert witnesses satisfies these factors, a board member is left with basing his decision on the credibility of the expert witness.

Determining the credibility of an expert witness is similar to determining the credibility of people in our daily lives:

- Was the expert witness candid about difficult aspects of his testimony? Did the expert witness admit the gray areas or did the expert witness attempt to gloss over anything that might be detrimental to his position?

- Was the testimony of the expert witness clear or did the expert witness use jargon and terms only understandable to members of his profession?

- Did the expert witness make good eye contact? Is the expert witness trustworthy?

A board member should apply a similar analysis when evaluating the credibility of a layperson.

It should be noted that remarks made by an attorney on behalf of a party are generally not considered evidence for the board's consideration. Rather, such remarks are simply arguments about the facts and law associated with a pending application. Accordingly, a board member should not base factual determinations on the remarks of an attorney.

DOCUMENTARY EVIDENCE

How to Evaluate Documentary Evidence

The concerns about how to evaluate a witness usually do not exist with documentary evidence (e.g., staff reports and photographs). Typically, documentary evidence is submitted to the board during the testimony of a witness. A board member should review the documentary evidence and ask questions if clarification is needed from the witness who presented the evidence.

Oftentimes, the volume of documentary evidence will be so great that the board may need to adjourn the hearing so the board members can review it. Such an adjournment may be for 10 to 15 minutes or until the next regularly scheduled meeting. The key is to provide adequate time for each board member to review and understand the documentary evidence.

In most states, the rules of evidence do not apply during a hearing conducted before a board. The board may, however, adopt rules to determine the kind of documentary evidence that will be received.

One kind of documentary evidence that is not entitled to any weight or consideration by the board is a petition for or against a pending application. As previously stated, all layperson testimony must be fact based (e.g., a petition that simply states that 100 people oppose or support the pending application is not fact based). Accordingly, such a petition is not considered to be "competent" evidence (also referred to as "substantial" evidence). The board must base its decisions upon competent evidence and not on opinion polls.

This same principle applies when the room is packed with people for or against a pending application. The number of people for or against a proposal is nothing more than an opinion poll, which is irrelevant to the board's obligation to base its decision on the competent evidence provided during the hearing.

SWORN TESTIMONY

Many jurisdictions require that a witness be placed under oath prior to testifying during the hearing. Just like a regular court proceeding, placing a witness under oath helps to ensure that the witness will provide truthful testimony. It also reinforces the gravity of the issue pending before the board.

Two approaches are commonly used for placing witnesses under oath:

1. At the beginning of the hearing on a pending application, the chair of the board instructs all people who intend to testify to stand and be placed under oath. An oath is then taken by all potential witnesses at one time. If this approach is used, it is important to ask each witness at the beginning of his testimony whether he was placed under oath, because some witnesses may arrive late and miss the group swearing in.

2. The safest and more preferable approach is to place each witness under oath once the witness is prepared to testify. This approach does not take any more time than the first approach because the first approach requires each witness to be asked whether he was present for the "group swearing in." By the time that question is asked and answered, the witness could already be placed under oath.

CROSS-EXAMINATION AND RIGHT OF REBUTTAL

Parties in a hearing before the board have a right to ask questions of a witness who has testified before the board, which is called "cross-examination." The purpose of cross-examination is to subject evidence to close scrutiny to establish its truthfulness.

Cross-examination is not an opportunity to launch personal attacks against a witness, and must focus upon the issues raised during the testimony of that witness. The chair of the board should limit inappropriate cross-examination.

In a contested proceeding, each side has the right to present evidence that rebuts the testimony of the other side. This right can, however, be abused. Therefore, the board has the legal authority to impose reasonable time restrictions upon such testimony.

What is reasonable varies from case to case. If a pending application raises several technical issues, which require the testimony of multiple expert witnesses, a board may need to schedule several hours for the hearing. Indeed, in particularly contentious and complex cases, it is common for the hearing to last more than one night. When that occurs, the board should make every effort to accommodate the scheduling needs of all of the parties involved, including the witnesses and their attorneys.

QUESTIONING OF WITNESSES
BY BOARD MEMBERS

It is appropriate for a board member to ask a witness a few questions to clarify the testimony of that witness. It is important to remember, however, that a board member is not an advocate for one side or the other, nor is a board member a prosecutor. Consequently, such questions must be asked in a respectful and polite manner. If a board member, or the board as a whole, asks questions in an argumentative, hostile, or disrespectful manner, it is possible that a court will invalidate the board's decision bcause such conduct demonstrates that the board member or board was biased against the party for whom such witness was testifying.

It is often suggested that board members wait until all witnesses have testified before asking any questions. This approach should not be used. It is difficult to remember questions for witnesses who may have testified a few hours ago. Even if a board member writes down his questions, a long delay before asking the question oftentimes results in confusion because the context in which the question arose has long passed.

As long as the questions are brief, designed to elicit clarification, and asked in a polite manner, there is nothing wrong with a board member asking a witness questions while that witness is testifying. Whenever a board member asks a question, however, all parties involved in the hearing must be allowed an opportunity to ask follow-up questions of the witness if they desire.

A Nevada Experience

The criteria for a variance in Nevada include demonstration of a hardship. The hardship must be related to the shape or topography of the lot, resulting in a loss of use of the land. Michael Harper, currently the Planning Manager in Washoe County, Nevada, reports the following unusual findings in one case during his 23-year career with boards of adjustment:

"An applicant submitted a request to increase the height of a detached garage to accommodate additional habitable space over the garage. The existing garage was located near the street.

"Staff recommended denial of the variance, due to lack of a demonstrated hardship. Further, granting the variance would result in shading the street during icy conditions.

"During the public hearing, only the applicant spoke, and provided attractive pictures of the garage addition. At the close of the public hearing, a member of the board declared that she knew the applicant to be an upstanding citizen of the community. She further stated that the additional height was an attractive addition and that no one in the neighborhood came forward to oppose the variance.

"The board then approved the variance. When queried by staff as to what findings should be stated to support the approval, the board adopted the following finding: 'no opposition from the neighbors.'"

Don't do this. It is not an appropriate finding.

FINDINGS OF FACT AND CONCLUSIONS OF LAW

In most jurisdictions, the board is required to enter a written decision, which contains "findings of fact" and "conclusions of law." The board's written decision must be supported by the competent evidence that was presented during the hearing on the pending application.

The findings of fact are the factual determinations made by the board in reaching its decision. This is where the board states which of the conflicting evidence it has determined to be the most credible. The findings of fact should include a summary of the evidence presented at the hearing.

The conclusions of law are the conclusions that the board reaches after applying the applicable law to the pending application. For example, if the local government's regulations contain criteria for the granting of a conditional use, this is the section of the written order in which the board sets forth its conclusions regarding the applicant's compliance with such criteria.

A copy of the board's written order should be mailed to the applicant and all parties who participated in the board's hearing. Additionally, a copy should be placed in the application file. This is especially important if the board placed conditions upon its approval. By placing a copy in the application file, staff can monitor whether the applicant has fulfilled the conditions. (Chapter 5 has further discussion on record keeping.)

THE ROLE OF THE
BOARD ATTORNEY

It is common for a board to utilize the services of an attorney. A board attorney can help the board avoid violating the due process rights of the parties who appear before the board. Similarly, a board attorney can provide useful advice regarding questions about evidence that is presented during a hearing.

It is important to remember, however, that the board attorney only provides advice to the board. In other words, the board attorney is not a decision-maker. The board retains the ultimate authority to follow or reject the board attorney's advice.

For example, sometimes a party may raise an objection to the admissibility of evidence being presented by a witness. Most board members do not have the legal training to evaluate the admissibility of evidence. Under such circumstances, it is typical for the board to look to the board attorney for guidance regarding how to rule upon an objection. It is appropriate for the board attorney to recommend to the board chair whether to sustain or overrule the objection, but the final decision to do so clearly lies with the board.

Some boards allow the chair to rule upon objections, subject to being overruled by a vote of the majority of the board; other boards vote as a body on each objection. Although there is no legal requirement that mandates either of these approaches, the first approach is more expeditious.

It is beneficial for each board member to meet privately with the board attorney when the board member begins his term. The board attorney can provide the board member with an overview of the board's procedures. Additionally, the board attorney can help explain the due process concerns that are addressed in this chapter (see also Chapter 8). This meeting provides an opportunity for the board attorney and the board member to discuss their expectations regarding how a board meeting should be conducted.

THE FLOW OF A
QUASI-JUDICIAL HEARING

Figure 9-1 is a flow chart describing the sequence of events and an overview of the procedures that should be followed during a quasi-judicial hearing. Prior to utilizing the flow chart, the board should consult with the board attorney to determine whether the content of the flow chart is consistent with the legal requirements of the state or local government in which the board is located.

Figure 9-1. The Flow of a Quasi-Judicial Hearing

Chair announces first item for board consideration

/ Board members disclose any ex parte communication
/ Any party[1] may inquire about any ex parte communication

Staff presentation

/ Staff member is placed under oath
/ Staff member provides an overview and analysis of item
/ Staff member is cross-examined[2]

Applicant presentation

/ Party's first witness[3] is placed under oath
/ Testimony[4] is given by witness
/ Witness is cross-examined
/ Follow-up questions are asked to clarify testimony during cross-examination
(Repeat sequence for each witness)

Opponent presentation
(There may be either no opposition or one or more opponents; the same process applies to each opponent who wishes to present evidence)

Applicant rebuttal

Public comment[5]

Chair announces closure of evidentiary portion of the hearing

Motion to approve, to approve with conditions, or to deny

If motion is seconded, board members may discuss the motion

Chair asks the board to vote; vote is taken

The hearing is concluded on that item and the board moves on to the next matter or closes the hearing

1. A party is a person who has a specific interest in the matter being considered by the board. Each state or local government will have specific requirements to determine who is a party to the matter. The issue of who is a party should be discussed with the board attorney and made a part of the rules and procedures for board actions.

2. Cross-examination may be by a lay person who is a party or an attorney representing a party to the matter.

3. The applicant or opponent may also be the witness and may be the only witness.

4. Testimony may be in a question-and-answer format, with the applicant or applicant's attorney asking questions or a presentation by the witness.

5. The board should not rely upon public comment in reaching its decision, unless such comment is under oath and subject to cross-examination.

Glossary

Access management: the process of providing and managing access to land development while preserving the regional flow of traffic in terms of safety, capacity, and speed.

Administrative decision: any decision made by the senior administrative official, such as the director of community development or his or her designee.

Applicant: a property owner or any person or entity acting as an agent for the property owner in an application for a development proposal, permit, or approval.

Bulk: the size and mutual relationships of a building or structure and the location of same with respect to: size and height of the building; location of exterior walls at all levels in relation to lot lines, streets, or other buildings; gross floor area of the building in relation to the lot area; and all open space allocated to the building.

Bylaws: rules adopted by a board which govern its procedures regarding the use.

By right: uses permissible so long as they conform to the design requirements for the district.

Capital improvement: any building or infrastructure project that will be owned by a governmental unit and purchased or built with direct appropriations from the governmental unit, or with bonds backed by its full faith and credit, or, in whole or in part, with federal or other public funds, or in any combination thereof.

Character: special physical characteristics of a structure or area that set it apart from its surroundings and contribute to its individuality.

Compatibility: design which utilizes accepted site planning and the elements of architectural composition within the context of the surrounding area; a condition where adjacent and nearby buildings, activities, and uses of land fit together in a way to achieve balance and harmony in the neighborhood.

Compliance: consistent with the requirements of state statutes, the state comprehensive plan, the appropriate regional policy plan, the local comprehensive plan, and/or local regulations.

Comprehensive plan: the adopted official statement of a legislative body of a local government that sets forth goals, policies, and guidelines intended to direct the present and future physical, social, and economic development that occurs within its planning jurisdiction, and that includes a unified physical design for the public and private development of land and water.

Concurrency: installation and operation of facilities and services needed to meet the demands of new development simultaneous with the development.

Conditional use: a use or occupancy of a structure, or a use of land, permitted only upon issuance of a conditional use permit and subject to the limitations and conditions specified therein.

Drainage: surface water runoff; the removal of surface water or groundwater from land by drains, grading, or other means that include runoff controls to minimize erosion and sedimentation during and after construction or development, the means for preserving the water supply, and the prevention or alleviation of flooding.

Due process of law: a requirement that legal proceedings be carried out in accordance with established rules and principles.

Extraterritorial land use controls: authority granted to certain cities to exercise zoning and subdivision powers for a specified distance outside their boundaries.

General plan: a comprehensive declaration of goals, policies, and programs for the development of the city or county and including, where applicable, diagrams, maps, and text setting forth objectives, principles, standards, and other features, and which has been adopted by the governing body.

Habitat: the physical location or type of environment in which an organism or biological population lives or occurs.

Hardship: a restriction on property so unreasonable that it results in an arbitrary and capricious interference with basic property rights.

Hearing examiner: a public official who usually has authority to hold public hearings in connection with applications for variances, special use permits, and small parcel rezonings, and, occasionally, has the authority to make approval or denial decisions.

Impact: the effect of any direct man-made actions on existing physical, social, or economic conditions.

Intensity: relative measure of development impact as defined by characteristics such as the number of dwelling units per acre, amount of traffic generated, and amount of site coverage.

Land development regulation: any zoning, subdivision, impact fee, site plan, corridor map, floodplain or stormwater regulations, or other governmental controls that affect the use, density, intensity, or design development.

Landscaping: the bringing of the soil surface to a smooth finished grade, installing sufficient trees, shrubs, ground cover, and grass to soften building lines, provide shade, and generally produce a pleasing visual effect of the premises.

Land use plan: the long-range plan for the desirable use of land in the city or county as officially adopted and as amended from time to time by an elected or appointed body.

Lot coverage: a measure of intensity of land use that represents the portion of a site that is impervious (e.g., does not absorb water).

Master plan: a comprehensive long-range plan intended to guide growth and development of a community or region and one that includes analysis, recommendation, and proposals for the community's population economy, housing, transportation, community facilities, and land use.

Neighborhood: an area of a community with characteristics that distinguish it from other community areas and that may include schools, social clubs, or boundaries defined by physical barriers, such as major highways and railroads, or natural features, such as rivers.

NIMBY (Not In My Backyard): refers to the situation where people object to a use or development that they feel should be located elsewhere.

Nonconforming illegal structure: a structure that did not legally exist prior to the adoption of an ordinance or regulation and does not conform with the current ordinance requirements for the district in which it is located.

Nonconforming use: a use that was valid when brought into existence but by subsequent regulation becomes no longer conforming (e.g., a structure, use, or parcel of land).

Nuisance: any thing, condition, or conduct that endangers health and safety, or unreasonably offends the senses, obstructs the free use and comfortable enjoyment of property, or essentially interferes with the comfortable enjoyment of life.

Ordinance: a law or regulation set forth and adopted by a governmental authority, usually a city or county.

Planned unit development: a description of a proposed unified development, consisting, at a minimum, of a map and adopted ordinance setting forth the regulations governing, and the location and phasing of all proposed uses and improvements to be included in the development.

Planning commission: a board of the local government consisting of such elected and/or appointed members whose functions include advisory or nontechnical aspects of planning and may also include such other powers and duties as may be assigned to it by the legislative body.

Plat: a map representing a tract of land, showing the boundaries and location or individual properties and streets; a map, a subdivision, or a site plan.

Pollution: the presence of matter or energy whose nature, location, or quantity produces undesired environmental effects.

Public hearing: a meeting announced and advertised in advance and open to the general public wherein the public has an opportunity to comment and participate.

Quasi-judicial decision: similar to a court proceeding where affected parties are afforded more procedural safeguards; the process is characteristic of most meetings of a planning commission or board of adjustment.

Redevelopment: any proposed expansion, addition, or major façade change to an existing building, structure, or parking facility.

Rezoning: a change in the district boundaries or the zoning classification for a parcel.

Sense of place: the constructed and natural landmarks and social and economic surroundings that cause someone to identify with a particular place or community.

Setback: the minimum distance by which any building or structure must be separated from a street right-of-way or lot line.

Site plan: a drawing showing existing and proposed conditions including locations and dimensions of buildings, structures, pavements, landscaping, and natural features.

Site plan review: the review of the site plan of any public or private project by the department of planning or the planning commission.

Smart growth: development that enhances existing communities, is compatible with the natural environment, and uses tax dollars efficiently while attracting private investment.

Special use: a use that meets the intent and purpose of the zoning district but which requires the review and approval of the appropriate planning commission or board of adjustment in order to ensure that any adverse impacts on adjacent uses, structures, or public services and facilities that may be generated by the use can be, and are, mitigated.

Specimen tree: a tree designated by the local government due to size, age, or historical significance.

Subdivision regulation: the control of the division of a tract of land by requiring development according to design standards and procedures adopted by local ordinance.

Topography: the physical land surface relief describing the terrain elevation and slope.

Tree, canopy: any self-supporting woody plant or a species that normally achieves an overall height at maturity of 30 feet or more.

Trip generation: the dynamics that account for people making trips in automobiles or by means of public transportation.

Use: any purpose for which a lot, building, or other structure or a tract of land may be designated, arranged, intended, maintained, or occupied; of any activity, occupation, business, or operation carried on or intended to be carried on in a building or other structure or on a tract of land.

Variance: permission to depart from development regulations when, because of special circumstances applicable to the property, strict application of the provisions of the regulations deprives such property of privileges enjoyed by other property in the vicinity that is under identical zoning.

Waiver: permission to depart from development regulations or procedures.

Wetland: those areas that are inundated and saturated by surface or ground-water at a frequency and duration sufficient to support, and that under normal circumstances do support, a prevalence of vegetation typically adapted for life in saturated soil conditions, including swamps, marshes, bogs, and similar areas.

Zoning: the division of a city or county by legislative regulations into areas, or zones, which specify allowable uses for real property and size restrictions for buildings within these areas; a program that implements policies of the general plan.

Sample Staff Reports
and Written Order

Appendix A:
Sample Staff Report for a Special Use

The following is a staff report and action taken on a special-use permit application for a coastal community in Florida.

APPLICATION INFORMATION

Applicant and owner	(owner's name)
Agent	(agent's name)
Requested action	Approval of a special use for remodeling a structure and the addition of a second story and a garage
Location	(property address), within the Coastal High Hazard Area (CHHA), within the Beach Overlay District, and both landward and seaward of the coastal construction control line
Existing zoning	R-2
Future land use map category	Medium density residential
Size	Approximately .45 acre

All required application materials have been received. All fees have been paid. All required notices have been made.

SURROUNDING AREA INFORMATION

Adjacent zoning	R-2 on north, south, and west; beach and Atlantic Ocean to the east
Adjacent future land use map category	Medium density residential on the north, south, and west

SUMMARY OF REQUEST AND BACKGROUND INFORMATION

The property is located in the CHHA. Development within the CHHA is only allowable through the special use permit process (§ 110-31, Land Development Code). An existing, one-story residential structure is proposed for remodeling and expansion through the addition of a second story and a garage. The new garage replaces the existing garage, which is proposed for conversion to a bedroom and bath. Both the existing garage and the proposed new garage are located landward of the coastal construction setback line. The second-story addition is proposed over the existing footprint and lies both landward and seaward of the coastal construction setback line.

The surrounding area consists of similar construction, a mixture of one- and two-story structures.

CONSISTENCY WITH THE COMPREHENSIVE PLAN

• *Conservation and Coastal Management Element (CCME) Policy 5a.02.07* requires that the City adopt land development regulations governing development adjacent to the Atlantic shoreline.

The City has adopted regulations as required. These regulations are contained in Chapter 110, Article II, of the Land Development Code, and apply to this site. The regulations are discussed below.

• *CCME Policy 5a.03.01* requires that the future land use map not allow any increase in the net development capacity within the CHHA.

The proposal is for remodeling and additions to an existing structure. There is no proposed increase in net development capacity. The site plan and floor plan submitted with the development application indicate that the structure will continue to be a single-family house.

• *CCME Policy 5a.07.06* and *Future Land Use Element Policy 1.06.08* define the CHHA as the category 1 hurricane evacuation zone.

This site lies within the CHHA and is, therefore, subject to policies pertaining to development within the CHHA, as listed herein.

• *CCME Policy 5a.07.07* establishes that development may be allowed within the CHHA, but that there should be no increase in the net development capacity within the CHHA.

As indicated above, the proposed remodeling and additions do not result in an increase in the net development capacity within the CHHA, as measured by density.

• *Future Land Use Element Policy 1-2.01.02* provides that medium-density residential areas shall be provided for development and redevelopment, and maintained for stable residential development.

The site is within the medium-density residential land use category and is within a stable residential area, where existing structures are maintained and redevelopment similar to that proposed in this application occurs.

CONSISTENCY WITH THE LAND DEVELOPMENT CODE

• § 110-92 (Land Development Code) lists permitted activities within the coastal protection zone (the CHHA). § 110-92(b)(7) provides that uses permitted by the zoning classification that have "all necessary and valid permits from state, federal and local government agencies have permitting jurisdiction" are permitted.

The single-family dwelling is an allowable use in the R-2 zoning district.

- § 110-93 (Land Development Code) lists the conditions for approval of special permit uses.

The use itself, a single-family dwelling, is existing. However, the following is a summary of the consistency of the application with the required conditions:

(1) The activity is water dependent or water related.

The proposal is for remodeling and additions to an existing dwelling. Therefore, this condition does not apply, as a new use is not being established.

(2) No practical use is possible for the entire parcel of land owned by the applicant and alternative locations outside of the coastal protection zone are not available.

The proposal is for remodeling and additions to an existing dwelling. A new use is not being established. Therefore, this condition does not apply.

(3) The use will not threaten public safety or cause nuisances, increase flooding on other lands, impair public rights to the enjoyment or plant or animal species, or violate pollution control standards or other federal, state, or local regulations. In addition, the use must be protected against flooding, erosion and other hazards.

The proposal does not increase development capacity, as measured by density, nor does it include any new impervious surface seaward of the coastal construction control line. The use is required to comply with any building standards applicable to remodeling and building additions, and, therefore, complies with this condition.

(4) The public benefit of the proposed use, unequivocally, far outweighs any loss of or damage to public resources.

There is no loss or damage to public resources. Therefore, there is neither a public benefit nor a public loss, based on evaluation of resources. Improvement to the structure is similar to improvements to other beachfront structures in the area and contributes to the maintenance of a stable neighborhood. A stable neighborhood is a public benefit.

(5) The proposed use will not, when viewed by itself and in terms of the cumulative impact of existing and reasonably anticipated future uses of a similar nature, result in

(a) Dredging and filling of the wetlands or other modification of natural topographic contours;

There is no proposed dredging and filling of wetlands or modification of contours; therefore, this condition is met.

(b) Significant disturbance or destruction of natural flora and fauna;

There is no proposed disturbance or destruction of natural flora and fauna; therefore, this condition is met.

(c) Significant increases in water turbidity due to influx of sediments or other materials;
(d) Substantial removal of wetland soils;
(e) Reduction or increases in wetland water supply;
(f) Influx of toxic chemicals; and
(g) Thermal changes in the wetlands.

There are no wetlands associated with this site; therefore, these conditions do not apply.

(6) All other federal, state and local permits have been obtained, so long as the city commission received adequate advance notice prior to the owner applying for such permits.

A letter dated April 16, 2004, has been received from the Florida Department of Environmental Protection (DEP). This letter documents a determination that the proposed work is exempt from the environmental permitting requirements of the Florida DEP. The DEP determination is based on the proposed additions seaward of the coastal construction control line being contained within the footprint of the existing one-story building. The determination is also based on the following conditions:

> **"Provided that the existing foundations are unaltered, that no habitable space is constructed seaward of the existing habitable space (ie. [sic] No enclosure and/or second story addition to the existing seaward wood deck), that all demolition debris is removed to a location seaward of the control line, and that construction does not impact due features or native vegetation. . . ."**

CONCLUSION

The requested special use permit is consistent with the applicable sections of the Comprehensive Plan and the Land Development Code.

RECOMMENDATION

Approve the special use permit, conditioned upon compliance with the conditions described in the DEP letter as noted above.

During the public hearing, a staff member summarized the report, stated the staff recommendation, and responded to clarifying questions from members of the board. The agent for the applicant stated his agreement with the staff report and gave a brief overview of the proposed project. Board members asked questions to verify their understanding of the application and the staff report. No members of the public spoke regarding this application.

The board attorney stated for the record that the board had competent substantial evidence with regard to the application. The board voted unanimously to recommend approval to the City Commission. In this community, final authority for a special use rests with the City Commission.

Appendix B:
Sample Staff Report for a Variance

REPORT AND RECOMMENDATION

To:	Board of Adjustment
From:	Community Development Director
Subject:	VAR-2004-01
Date:	January 3, 200X
Meeting Date:	January 10, 200X

ISSUE/BACKGROUND

Applicant:	Mr. Developer, on behalf of XYZ Development, Inc. (owner)
Location:	City of Somewhere, USA
Zoning:	Residential Intensive Apartment ("RIA") zoning district
Future Land Use:	Mixed Use ("MU")
Legal Notice:	The request for a variance was advertised in the *Daily News* on December 30, 200X.
Applicant's Request:	Mr. Developer, on behalf of XYZ Development, Inc. (owner), is requesting a variance from Sections 11.05.01(E) and (F) of the City's Land Development Code ("LDC") to allow for the extension of a dock beyond the maximum allowed distance of 200 feet.

DISCUSSION/FINDINGS

Sections 11.05.01(E) and (F) of the LDC require that all piers not extend into the City Harbor by more than 200 feet:

> Section 11.05.01(E): No new or existing dock shall be constructed or modified such that the length of any pier as completed is greater than 20 percent of the width of the harbor at the place where the pier is located, or out 200 feet, whichever is less.

> Section 11.05.01(F): No piling(s) shall be added to the waterward end of any pier which piling(s) would make the total length of the dock more than 200 feet.

It is important to note that Section 11.05.00 of the LDC limits other elements of the construction of docks within the City Harbor. One of the

more significant requirements is contained in Section 11.05.01(J): "No dock shall be constructed such that it constitutes a hazard to navigation."

According to Section 21-73 of the LDC, the Board of Adjustment ("BOA") is required to make six (6) specific findings in order to approve a variance request. These findings are listed below along with staff's analysis.

1. **That special conditions or circumstances exist which are peculiar to the land, structure, or building involved and which are not applicable to other lands, structures, or buildings in the same zoning district.**

    Staff Analysis: Special conditions or circumstances regarding this site, which do not exist for other sites that abut the City Harbor and with the same zoning district, are not present. All properties along the City Harbor have sea grasses and oyster beds in the areas where docks are typically constructed.

2. **That special conditions and circumstances do not result from the actions of the applicant.**

    Staff Analysis: The applicant contends that the following facts constitute special circumstances, which are not a result of its actions:

    A. The sea grasses and oyster beds existed prior to the applicant's ownership; and

    B. The location and design of the dock are based upon efforts to preserve the sea grasses and oyster beds.

    The proposed dock could be redesigned to protect the sea grasses and the oyster beds, and still comply with the 200-foot limitation. Therefore, staff has not found any special conditions or circumstances that do not result from the actions of the applicant.

3. **That granting the variance requested would not confer on the applicant any special privileges denied by any zoning ordinance to other lands, buildings, or structures in the same zoning district.**

    Staff Analysis: The granting of this variance would confer a special privilege to the applicant, due to the fact that all lots within the same zoning district are required to satisfy the same 200-foot maximum length requirement.

4. **That literal interpretation of the provisions of any zoning ordinance would deprive the applicant of rights commonly enjoyed by other properties in the same zoning district under the terms of any zoning ordinance, and would work unnecessary and undue hardship on the applicant.**

    Staff Analysis: The literal interpretation does not deprive the applicant of rights commonly enjoyed by others in the same zoning district, due to the fact that the applicant can construct a dock which complies with the 200-foot maximum length requirement.

5. **That the variance granted is the minimum variance that would make possible the reasonable use of the land, building, or structure.**

   Staff Analysis: This is not the minimum variance possible, due to the fact that the applicant can redesign the proposed dock to protect the sea grasses and oyster beds and still comply with the 200-foot limitation.

6. **That the granting of the variance would be in harmony with the general intent and purpose of any zoning ordinance, and that such variance would not be injurious to the area involved or otherwise detrimental to the public welfare.**

   Staff Analysis: The proposed design would create a navigational hazard.

STAFF'S CONCLUSION

The applicant has failed to meet all six (6) criteria for granting a variance. Therefore, staff is unable to support this variance request.

Note: Staff has received no letters of opposition or support for the requested variance.

RECOMMENDATION

Staff recommends that the Board of Adjustment **deny** the requested variance.

RECOMMENDED MOTION

It is moved to **deny** the requested variance.

Appendix C:
Sample Final Order for a Variance

BEFORE THE BOARD OF ADJUSTMENT
FOR CITY OF SOMEWHERE, USA

In Re: Variance Requested By Development, Inc.

FINAL ORDER

This matter came before the Board of Adjustment ("Board") for hearing on <date>, pursuant to proper notice published in accordance with the City's Land Development Code ("LDC"). Based upon the evidence presented during the quasi-judicial hearing, the Board renders the following Findings of Fact and Conclusions of Law:

Findings of Fact

1. Development, Inc., is requesting a variance from the requirements of Sections 11.05.01(E) and (F) of the City's LDC in order to build a dock in excess of the 200-foot maximum length requirement. The applicant seeks a dock that is 250 feet long. The basis for the applicant's request is that the variance is needed to protect sea grasses and oyster beds. The applicant presented the testimony of its engineer in support of its request.

2. The City staff presented evidence in opposition to the applicant's request. Such evidence indicated that the applicant could construct a dock within the 200-foot maximum limit imposed by Sections 11.05.01(E) and (F) of the City's LDC and still protect the sea grasses and the oyster beds.

3. The City staff also presented evidence which demonstrated that a dock beyond the 200-foot maximum limit would threaten the safety of boaters who utilize the waterway. Although the applicant presented evidence to the contrary, the Board finds the City staff's testimony and evidence to be more credible and persuasive.

4. The applicant's engineer admitted during cross-examination that it was possible to construct a dock within the 200-foot maximum limit imposed by Sections 11.05.01(E) and (F) of the City's LDC. However, such a dock would not be configured in a manner that was as desirable as the one for which the applicant seeks a variance.

5. Pursuant to Section 21-73 of the City's LDC, an applicant must demonstrate that he is entitled to a variance by complying with each of the following criteria:

    A. That special conditions or circumstances exist which are peculiar to the land, structure, or building involved, and which are not applicable to other lands, structures, or buildings in the same zoning district.

    B. That special conditions and circumstances do not result from the actions of the applicant.

    C. That granting the variance will not confer on the applicant any special privileges denied by any zoning ordinance to other lands, buildings, or structures in the same zoning district.

    D. That literal interpretation of the provisions of any zoning ordinance would deprive the applicant of rights commonly enjoyed by other properties in the same zoning district under the terms of a zoning ordinance, and would work unnecessary and undue hardship on the applicant.

    E. That the variance granted is the minimum variance that will make possible the reasonable use of the land, building, or structure.

    F. That the granting of the variance will be in harmony with the general intent and purpose of any zoning ordinance and that such variance will not be injurious to the area involved or otherwise detrimental to the public welfare.

6. The Board finds that the applicant has failed to demonstrate that special circumstances exist on the applicant's property to warrant the granting of the requested variance. Indeed, the applicant has conceded that it is possible to construct a dock without exceeding the 200-foot maximum limit and still protect the sea grasses and the oyster beds. The applicant's desire for a "nicer" dock does not constitute a hardship.

7. The Board further finds that a dock beyond the 200-foot maximum length would create a public safety threat. The location of such a dock would create a navigational hazard.

Conclusions of Law

8. The Board concludes that the applicant has failed to fulfill the criteria of Section 21-73 of the City's LDC. The applicant failed to demonstrate that it is not possible to construct a dock without exceeding the 200-foot maximum limit and still protect the sea grasses and the oyster beds. The applicant's desire for a "nicer" dock does not constitute a hardship.

9. Moreover, the Board concludes that the potential threat to the safety of boaters who utilize the waterway provides an independent basis for

denial of the applicant's request for a variance. Protection of the public's health, safety, and welfare is of paramount importance to this Board.

10. Consequently, the Board concludes that the applicant has failed to fulfill criteria A, C, D, and F above.

11. Accordingly, the variance requested by Development, Inc., is hereby **DENIED.**

This Order is final and effective as of the date of filing with the City Clerk as indicated below.

DONE AND APPROVED BY A MAJORITY OF THE BOARD MEMBERS PRESENT AND VOTING AT THE EVIDENTIARY HEARING IN THIS MATTER on the 10th day of January 200X.

_____

Chairperson

Filed this ____ day of _____.

_____

Deputy Clerk

Index